Modern One-act Plays

Tom Stoppard • James Saunders •
Harold Pinter

Modern One-act Plays

Edited by
Horst Buss, Bruno von Lutz and
Kunibert Schäfer

Ernst Klett Sprachen
Stuttgart

Tom Stoppard • James Saunders • Harold Pinter

Modern One-act Plays

Edited by Horst Buss, Bruno von Lutz and Kunibert Schäfer

Acknowledgements
H. Pinter, *A Slight Ache* from *A Slight Ache and Other Plays* (1961) is reprinted by permission of Eyre Methuen Ltd., London.
J. Saunders, *A Slight Accident* from *Neighbours and Other Plays* (1964) is reprinted by permission of Andre Deutsch Ltd., London.
T. Stoppard, *A Separate Peace* from *Playbill Two*, ed. Alan Durband, 1969, is reprinted by permission of Fraser & Dunlop Scripts Ltd., London.

1. Auflage   1   15 14 13 12 11 | 2028 27 26 25 24

Nachfolger von 978-3-12-578300-3
Alle Drucke dieser Auflage sind unverändert und können im Unterricht nebeneinander verwendet werden.
Die letzte Zahl bezeichnet das Jahr des Druckes. Das Werk und seine Teile sind urheberrechtlich geschützt. Jede Nutzung in anderen als den gesetzlich zugelassenen Fällen bedarf der vorherigen schriftlichen Einwilligung des Verlags.

© Ernst Klett Sprachen GmbH, Rotebühlstraße 77, 70178 Stuttgart, 1979. Alle Rechte vorbehalten. Die Nutzung der Inhalte für Text- und Data-Mining ist ausdrücklich vorbehalten und daher untersagt.

www.klett-sprachen.de

Unter Mitarbeit von Horst Buss, Bruno von Lutz, Kunibert Schäfer

Layoutkonzeption: Elmar Feuerbach
Gestaltung und Satz: Satzkasten, Stuttgart
Umschlaggestaltung: Sandra Vrabec
Titelbild: shutterstock.com, © Kevin Sprague, New York, NY
Druck und Bindung: Digitaldruck Tebben GmbH, Biessenhofen

Printed in Germany
ISBN 978-3-12-578301-0

Contents

Preface 6

Tom Stoppard *A Separate Peace* 7

Biographical Notes 49

James Saunders *A Slight Accident*......................... 51

Biographical Notes 82

Harold Pinter *A Slight Ache* 83

Biographical Notes 123

Glossary of Literary Terms 125

Preface

The theatre is one of the liveliest arts in modern Britain, and the last decades have seen a renaissance in the provincial theatre. Hand in hand with this new interest in drama, the one-act play has shown itself to be an adaptable and popular form.
The one-act plays in this collection are by three leading British dramatists.

The phonetic transcription in the *Annotations* is from Jones-Gimson, *English Pronouncing Dictionary*, 14th edition. The following abbreviations are used in the *Annotations:*

A.E.	American English	*poet.*	poetic
c.f.	confer, see	*sg.*	singular
coll.	*colloquial*	*sl.*	slang
etc.	*and so on, et cetera*	*s.o.*	*someone*
o.s.	*oneself*	*s.th.*	*something*
pl.	plural		

Numbers in bold-face type in the margin refer to the corresponding pages in the text, those in light-face type to the lines of the respective page.
Example: **4** 27 = page 4, line 27.

Tom Stoppard

A Separate Peace

Scene 1

(The office of the Beechwood Nursing Home. Behind the reception counter sits a uniformed nurse. It is 2.30 a.m. A car pulls up outside. John Brown enters. He is a biggish man in his late forties, with a well-lined face: calm, pleasant, implacable. He is wearing a nondescript suit and overcoat, and carrying two zipped grips. Looking around, he notes the neatness, the quiet, the flowers, the nice nurse, and is quietly pleased.)

BROWN Very nice.

NURSE Good evening …

BROWN 'Evening. A lovely night. Morning.

NURSE Yes … Mr …?

BROWN I'm sorry to be so late.

NURSE *(shuffling papers)* Were you expected earlier?

BROWN No. I telephoned.

NURSE Yes?

BROWN Yes.

NURSE I mean …?

BROWN You have a room for Mr Brown.

NURSE (realisation) Oh! – Have you brought him?

---

2 **nursing home** privately owned hospital – 3 **reception counter** desk where incoming patients are registered – 4 **to pull up** to come to a stop – 4 **biggish** rather big – 6 **implacable** [ɪmˈplækəbl] *here:* resolute, firm – 6 **nondescript** [ˈnɒndɪskrɪpt] ordinary looking – 7 **zipped grip** *(A.E.)* bag opened or closed by means of a zip-fastener – 15 **to shuffle** to move or push one over the other – 21 **realisation** realising what it means

BROWN I brought myself. Knocked up a taxi by the station.

NURSE *(puzzled)* But surely …?

BROWN I telephoned, from the station.

NURSE You said it was an emergency.

5 BROWN That's right. Do you know what time it is?

NURSE It's half past two.

BROWN That's right. An emergency.

NURSE *(aggrieved)* I woke the house doctor.

BROWN A kind thought. But it's all right. Do you want me to
10   sign in?

NURSE What is the nature of your emergency, Mr Brown?

BROWN I need a place to stay.

NURSE Are you ill?

BROWN No.

15 NURSE But this is a private hospital …

(Brown smiles for the first time.)

BROWN The best kind. What is a hospital without privacy? It's
the privacy I'm after – that and the clean linen … *(A thought
strikes him.)* I've got money.

20 NURSE … the Beechwood Nursing Home.

BROWN I require nursing. I need to be nursed for a bit. Yes.
Where do I sign?

---

1 **to knock up a taxi** to find a taxi – 8 **aggrieved** hurt in one's feelings – 10 **to sign in** to leave one's name and address with the receptionist – 17 **privacy** state of being undisturbed, secluded – 18 **to be after s.th.** to want s.th. badly – 19 **a thought strikes him** he suddenly has an idea

NURSE I'm sorry, but admissions have to be arranged in advance except in the case of a genuine emergency – I have no authority –

BROWN What do you want with authority? A nice girl like you. *(Moves)*

Where have you put me?

NURSE *(moves with him)* And *you* have no authority –

BROWN *(halts)* That's true. That's one thing I've never had. *(He looks at her flatly.)* I've come a long way.

NURSE *(wary)* Would you wait just one moment?

BROWN *(relaxes)* Certainly. Have you got a sign-in chit? Must abide by the regulations. Should I pay in advance?

NURSE No, that's quite all right.

BROWN I've got it – I've got it all in here –

(He starts trying to open one of the zipped cases, it jams and he hurts his finger. He recoils sharply and puts his finger in his mouth. The Doctor arrives, dishevelled from being roused.)

NURSE Doctor – this is Mr Brown.

DOCTOR Good evening. What seems to be the trouble?

BROWN Caught my finger.

DOCTOR May I see?

(Brown holds out his finger, the Doctor studies it, looks up. Guardedly)

---

1 **admission** [əd'mɪʃn] being allowed to enter or stay – 2 **genuine** ['dʒenjʊɪn] true – 3 **authority** right given to s.o. (in this case the right to admit new patients); power, the right to command – 9 **flatly** directly – 10 **wary** ['weərɪ] cautious – 11 **chit** form to be filled in – 12 **to abide by** [ə'baɪd] to obey – 15 **to jam** to get stuck – 16 **to recoil** to draw back in pain – 17 **dishevelled** [dɪ'ʃevld] with the hair in disorder – 18 **to rouse** s.o. [raʊz] to wake s.o. up – 24 **guardedly** cautiously

Have you come far?

BROWN Yes. I've been travelling all day.

(The Doctor glances at the nurse.)

BROWN Not with my finger. I did that just now. Zip stuck.

DOCTOR Oh. And what – er –

NURSE Mr Brown says there's nothing wrong with him.

BROWN That's right – I – –

NURSE He just wants a bed.

BROWN A room.

DOCTOR But this isn't a hotel.

BROWN Exactly.

DOCTOR Exactly what?

BROWN I don't follow you.

DOCTOR Perhaps I'm confused. You see, I was asleep.

BROWN It's all right. I understand. Well, if someone would show me to my room, I shan't disturb you any further.

DOCTOR *(with a glance at the nurse)* I don't believe we have any rooms free at the moment.

BROWN Oh yes, this young lady arranged it.

NURSE *(self-defence)* He telephoned from the station. He said it was an emergency.

BROWN I missed my connection.

DOCTOR But you've come to the wrong place.

---

22 **connection** train due to leave after the arrival of another train

BROWN No, this is the place all right. I don't want to be a nuisance.

DOCTOR Did you try the pubs in the town?

BROWN I'm not drunk.

DOCTOR They have rooms.

BROWN I've got a room. What's the matter?

DOCTOR *(pause)* Nothing – nothing's the matter. *(He nods at the nurse.)* All right.

NURSE Yes, doctor. *(Murmurs worriedly)* I'll have to make an entry …

DOCTOR Observation.

BROWN *(cheerfully)* I'm not much to look at.

NURSE Let me take those for you, Mr Brown. *(The cases)*

BROWN No, no, don't you. *(Picks up cases)* There's nothing the matter with me …

(Brown follows the nurse inside. The doctor watches them go, picks up Brown's form, and reads it. Then he picks up the phone and starts to dial.)

---

2 **nuisance** ['njuːsns] a troublesome person – 10 **to make an entry** *here:* to put s.o. on the list of patients and state for what purpose he is admitted

Scene 2

(Brown's private ward. A pleasant room with a hospital bed and the usual furniture. One wall is almost all window and is curtained. Brown and the nurse enter. Brown puts his cases on the bed. He likes the room.)

BROWN That's nice. I'll like it here.

NURSE Will you be all right?

BROWN Oh yes, I'm all right now. Picture window.

NURSE The bathroom is across the corridor.

BROWN *(peering through curtains)* What's the view?

NURSE Well, it's the drive and the gardens.

BROWN Gardens. A front room. What could be nicer?

(Nurse starts to open case.)

NURSE Are your night things in here?

BROWN Yes, I'll be very happy here.

(Nurse opens the case, which is full of money – bank notes.)

NURSE Oh — I'm sorry —

(Brown is not put out at all.)

BROWN What time is breakfast?

NURSE Eight o'clock.

BROWN Lunch?

NURSE Twelve o'clock.

BROWN Tea?

---

2 **ward** [wɔːd] room in a hospital – 8 **picture window** a large window with an attractive view – 10 **to peer** to look closely – 11 **drive** private road through a park or a garden – 18 **to be put out** to be offended

NURSE Three o'clock.

BROWN Supper?

NURSE Half past six.

BROWN Cocoa?

5 NURSE Nine.

BROWN Matron's rounds twice a day?

NURSE Yes.

BROWN Temperatures?

NURSE *(turning back his bed)* Morning and evening.

10 BROWN Change of sheets?

NURSE Monday.

BROWN Like clockwork. Lovely.

(The Doctor enters with Brown's form and Elastoplast.)

DOCTOR Excuse me.

15 BROWN I was just saying – everything's A1.

DOCTOR I remembered your finger.

BROWN I'd forgotten myself. It's nothing.

DOCTOR Well, we'll just put this on overnight.

(He administers Elastoplast.)

20 BROWN Must be wonderful to have the healing touch. I should get to bed now – you look tired.

DOCTOR Thank you, I expect matron will be along to discuss your case with you tomorrow.

---

6 **matron** ['meɪtrən] woman in charge of the nursing staff of hospital – 13 **Elastoplast** sticking-plaster – 15 **A1** first class – 19 **to administer** [əd'mɪnɪstə] to put on – 20 **the healing touch** ability to heal

BROWN My finger?

DOCTOR … Well, I expect she'd like to meet you.

BROWN Be pleased to meet her.

DOCTOR Yes … A final point, Mr Brown. This form you filled in … Where it says permanent address, you've put down Beechwood Nursing Home.

BROWN Yes. Well, you never know what the future brings, but for the while I like to think of it as home …

Scene 3

(The hospital office. It is morning, and the Doctor is at the desk, telephoning.)

DOCTOR   … I have absolutely no idea … The nurse said it looked like several hundred pounds … His savings, yes. Frankly, I wouldn't be too keen on that – I don't really want the police turning up at the bedside of any patient who doesn't arrive with a life history. . . . I think we'd get more out of him than you would, given a little time, and we'd certainly keep you informed … No, he's not being difficult at all … You don't need to worry about that – he doesn't seem very keen to run away. He seems quite happy …

---

6 **to be keen on** to be very interested in

Scene 4

(Brown's private ward. Brown is in striped pyjamas, eating off a tray. A second nurse – Nurse Coates (Maggie) – is waiting for him to finish so that she can take his tray away. Maggie is pretty and warm.)

BROWN The point is not breakfast in bed, but breakfast in bed without guilt. Rich men's wives can bring it off, but if you're not a rich man's wife then you've got to be ill. Lunch in bed is more difficult, even for the rich. It's not any more expensive, but the disapproval is harder to ignore. To stay in bed for tea is almost impossible in decent society, and not to get up at all would probably bring in the authorities. Even if you had the strength of character there's probably a point where it becomes certifiable. But in a hospital it's not only understood – it's expected. That's the beauty of it. I'm not saying it's a great discovery – it's obvious really: but I'd say I'd got something.

MAGGIE If you'd got something, there wouldn't be all this fuss.

BROWN Is there a fuss? *(Maggie doesn't answer.)* They should leave well alone. I'm paying my way … Are you pretty full all the time?

MAGGIE Not at the moment, not very.

BROWN You'd think a place as nice as this would be very popular.

MAGGIE Popular?

---

5 **warm** *here:* friendly – 7 **to bring s.th. off** to succeed in doing s.th. – 10 **disapproval** *here:* negative opinion – 11 **decent** ['diːsnt] respectable – 14 **certifiable** [ˌsɜːtɪ'faɪəbl] *here:* insane – 17 **I got something (there)** there is some truth in what I say – 18 **fuss** *(coll.)* confusion – 20 **to leave well alone** not to mind other people's business – 20 **I'm paying my way** I pay for everything I need

BROWN I thought I might have to wait for a place, you know. Of course, it's a bit out of the way, no passing trade, so to speak. I'm very fond of the English countryside myself.

MAGGIE Where do you live?

BROWN I've never lived. Only stayed.

MAGGIE You should settle down somewhere.

BROWN Yes, I've been promising myself this.

MAGGIE Have you got a family?

BROWN I expect so.

MAGGIE Where are they?

BROWN I lost touch.

MAGGIE You should find them.

BROWN *(smiles)* Their name's Brown.

(The matron enters: she is not too old, and quite equable.)

MATRON Good morning.

BROWN Good morning to you. You must be matron.

MATRON That's right.

BROWN I must congratulate you on your hospital, it's a lovely place you run here. Everyone is so nice.

MATRON Well, thank you, Mr Brown. I'm glad you feel at home.

(Maggie takes Brown's tray.)

BROWN I never felt it there. Very good breakfast. Just what the doctor ordered. I hope he got a bit of a lie-in.

---

2 **passing trade** customers who are attracted into a shop by the window display – 14 **equable** ['ɛkwəbl] friendly and patient – 24 **lie-in** staying in bed longer than usual

(Maggie exits with the tray, closing the door.)

MATRON Now, what's your problem, Mr Brown?

BROWN I have no problems.

MATRON Your complaint.

BROWN I have no complaints either. Full marks.

MATRON Most people who come here have something the matter with them. BROWN That must give you a lot of extra work.

MATRON But it's what we're here for. You see, you can't really stay unless there's something wrong with you.

BROWN I can pay.

MATRON That's not the point.

BROWN What is the point?

MATRON This is a hospital. What are you after?

BROWN *(sadly)* My approach is too straightforward. An ordinary malingerer or a genuine hypochondriac wouldn't have all this trouble. They'd be accepted on their own terms. All I get is a lot of personal questions. *(Hopefully)* Maybe I could catch something … But what difference would it make to you?

MATRON We have to keep the beds free for people who need them.

BROWN I need this room.

---

4 **complaint** illness, disease; grounds for dissatisfaction – 5 **full marks** everything is perfect – 12 **that's not the point** that's not what really matters – 15 **approach** method of doing something – 15 **straightforward** sincere, honest – 16 **malingerer** [məˈlɪŋgərə] person who *pretends* to be ill – 16 **hypochondriac** [ˌhaɪpəˈkɒndrɪæk] person who *thinks himself* to be ill – 17 **on their own terms** the way they are, as such

MATRON I believe you, Mr Brown – but wouldn't another room like this one do? – somewhere else? You see, we deal with physical matters – of the body -

BROWN There's nothing wrong with my mind. You won't find my name on any list.

MATRON I know.

BROWN *(teasing)* How do you know? *(She doesn't answer.)* Go for the obvious, it's worth considering. I know what I like: a nice atmosphere –good food – clean rooms – a day and night service – no demands – cheerful staff – Well, it's worth thirty guineas a week. I won't be any trouble.

MATRON Have you thought of going to a nice country hotel?

BROWN Different kettle of fish altogether. I want to do nothing, and have nothing expected of me. That isn't possible out there. It worries them. They want to know what you're at – staying in your room all the time – they want to know what you're doing. But in a hospital it is understood that you're not doing anything, because everybody's in the same boat – it's the normal thing. Being a patient. That's what I'm cut out for, I think – I've got a vocation for it.

MATRON But there's nothing wrong with you!

BROWN That's why I'm *here*. If there was something wrong with me I could get into any old hospital – free. As it is, I'm quite happy to pay for not having anything wrong with me. If I catch something, perhaps I'll transfer. I don't know, though. I like it here. It depends on how my money lasts. I wouldn't like to go to a city hospital.

MATRON But what do you want to do here?

---

7 to tease s.o. to make fun of s.o. playfully – **11 guinea** [ˈgɪnɪ] formerly 21 shillings (£1.05) – **13 a different kettle of fish** a completely different thing – **16 to be at s.th.** to intend to do s.th. – **20 to be cut out for s.th.** to be made for s.th. – **20 vocation** feeling that one is called to do a certain kind of work – **25 to transfer** [trænsˈfɜː] *here:* to move to another hospital

BROWN Nothing.

MATRON You'll find that very boring.

BROWN One must expect to be bored, in hospital.

MATRON Have you been in hospital quite a lot?

5 BROWN No. I've been saving up for it …

(He smiles.)

Scene 5

(The hospital office. The Doctor is phoning at a desk.)

DOCTOR No luck? … Oh. Well, I don't know. The only plan we've got is to bore him out of here, but he's disturbingly self-sufficient … Mmm, we've had a psychiatrist over … Well, he seemed amused … Both of them, actually; they were both amused … No, I shouldn't do that, he won't tell you anything. And there's one of our nurses – she's getting on very well with him … something's bound to come out soon …

---

5 **self-sufficient** [sə'fɪʃnt] needing no help from others

Scene 6

(Brown's ward. Brown is in bed with a thermometer in his mouth. Maggie is taking his pulse. She removes the thermometer, scans it and shakes it.)

5 MAGGIE I'm wasting my time here, you know.

BROWN *(disappointed)* Normal?

MAGGIE You'll have to do better than that if you're going to stay.

BROWN You're breaking my heart, Maggie.

10 MAGGIE *(almost lovingly)* Brownie, what are you going to do with yourself?

BROWN Maggie, Maggie … Why do you want me to do something?

MAGGIE They've all got theories about you, you know.

15 BROWN Theories?

MAGGIE Train-robber.

BROWN That's a good one.

MAGGIE A spy from the Ministry.

BROWN Ho ho.

20 MAGGIE Embezzler.

BROWN Naturally.

MAGGIE Eccentric millionaire.

BROWN Wish I was. I'd have my own hospital, just for myself. I'd have the whole thing – with wards all named after

---

4 **to scan** [skæn] to look at attentively – 20 **embezzler** [ɪmˈbezlə] a person who steals money placed in his care

dignitaries you've never heard of – and nurses, doctors, specialists, West Indian charladies, trolleys, rubber floors, sterilised aluminium, flowers, stretchers parked by the lifts, clean towels and fire regulations ... All built round me and staffed to feed me and check me and tick me off on a rota system.

MAGGIE It's generally agreed you're on the run.

BROWN No, I've stopped.

MAGGIE Fixations have been mentioned.

BROWN But you know better.

MAGGIE I think you're just lazy.

BROWN I knew you were the clever one.

MAGGIE *(troubled, soft)* Tell me what's the matter, Brownie?

BROWN I would if there was.

MAGGIE What do you want to stay here for then?

BROWN I like you.

MAGGIE You didn't know I was here.

BROWN That's true. I came for the quiet and the routine. I came for the white calm, meals on trays and quiet efficiency, time passing and bringing nothing. That seemed enough. I never got it down to a person. But I like you I like you very much.

MAGGIE Well, I like you too, Brownie. But there's more in life than that.

---

1 **dignitary** |ˈdɪgnɪtərɪ| person holding a high office – 2 **charlady** |ˈtʃɑːˌleɪdɪ| woman whose job it is to clean houses, hospitals, etc. – 2 **trolley** a table on small wheels for serving food – 3 **stretcher** a covered framework on which a sick person can be carried – 5 **staffed** equipped with personnel – 5 **to tick someone off** to put a small mark against names in a list – 6 **rota** list of persons who are to do things in turn – 7 **on the run** running away from the police etc. – 9 **fixation** *(in psychology)* abnormal feeling about, or love for, s.o. or s.th.

(Matron enters.)

MATRON Good morning.

BROWN Good morning, matron.

MATRON And how are we this morning?

BROWN We're very well. How are you?

MATRON *(slightly taken aback)* I'm all right, thank you. Well, are you enjoying life?

BROWN Yes thank you, matron.

MATRON What have you been doing?

BROWN Nothing.

MATRON And what do you want to do?

BROWN Nothing.

MATRON Now really, Mr Brown, this won't do, you know.

BROWN Why not?

MATRON You mustn't lose interest in life.

BROWN I was never very interested in the first place.

MATRON Wouldn't you like to get up for a while? Have a walk in the garden? There's no reason why you shouldn't.

BROWN No, I suppose not. But I didn't come here for that. I must have walked thousands of miles, in my time.

MATRON It's not healthy to stay in bed all day.

BROWN Perhaps I'll get something.

MATRON Well, isn't there anything you could do indoors?

BROWN What do the other patients do?

6 to be taken aback to be surprised

MATRON The other patients are here because they are not well.

BROWN I thought patients did things … *(vaguely)* Raffiawork …

5 MATRON Does that appeal to you?

BROWN No.

MATRON I suppose you wouldn't like to make paper flowers?

BROWN What on earth for? You've got lots of real ones.

MATRON You haven't got any.

10 BROWN Well, no one knows I'm here.

MATRON Then you must tell somebody.

BROWN I don't want them to know.

MATRON Who?

BROWN Everybody.

15 MATRON You'll soon get tired of sitting in bed.

BROWN Then I'll sit by the window. I'm easily pleased.

MATRON I can't let you just languish away in here. You must do something. BROWN *(sighs)* All right. What?

MATRON We've got basket-weaving … ?

20 BROWN Then I'll be left alone, will I?

---

3 **raffiawork** ['ræfiə] making baskets, hats, etc. from straw – 17 **to languish away** ['læŋgwɪʃ] to lose health and strength

Scene 7

(The hospital office. The doctor is on the phone.)

DOCTOR Well, I don't know – how many John Browns are there in Somerset House? … Good grief! … Of course, if it's any consolation it may not be his real name … I know it doesn't help … That's an idea, yes … His fingerprints … No, no, I'll get them on a glass or something – Well, he might have been in trouble some time …

---

4 **Somerset House** births, marriages and deaths used to be registered at Somerset House – 4 **good grief!** *(exclamation of surprise)* – 5 **consolation** comfort, relief

Scene 8

(Brown's ward. Brown is working on a shapeless piece of basketry. Matron enters.)

MATRON What is it?

BROWN Basketwork.

MATRON But what is it for?

BROWN Therapy.

MATRON You're making fun of me.

BROWN It is functional on one level only. If that. *You'd* like me to make a sort of laundry basket and lower myself in it out of the window. That would be functional on two levels. At least. *(Regards the mess sadly)* And I'm not even blind. Ladies and gentlemen – a failure! Now I suppose you'll start asking me questions again.

(Matron silently dispossesses Brown of his basketry.)

MATRON What about painting, Mr Brown?

(That strikes a chord.)

BROWN Painting … I used to do a bit of painting.

MATRON Splendid. Would you do some for me?

BROWN Paint in here?

MATRON Nurse Coates will bring you materials.

BROWN What colours do you like?

MATRON I like all colours. Just paint what you fancy. Paint scenes from your own life.

---

7 **therapy** ['θerəpɪ] – 10 **laundry** ['lɔːndrɪ] washing – 15 **to dispossess s.o. of s.th.** to take s.th. away from s.o. – 17 **to strike a chord** [kɔːd] to call up memories – 23 **to fancy** to like

BROWN Clever! Should I paint my last place of employment?

MATRON I'm trying to help you.

BROWN I'm sorry. I know you are. But I don't need help. Everything's fine for me. *(Pause)* Would you like me to paint English countryside?

MATRON Yes, that would be nice.

Scene 9

(The hospital office. The doctor is on the phone.)

DOCTOR No … well, we haven't got anything against him really. He's not doing any harm. No, he pays regularly. We can't really refuse … He's got lots left …

Scene 10

(Brown's ward. Brown is painting English countryside all over one wall. He hasn't got very far but one sees the beginnings of a simple pastoral panorama, competent but amateurish. Maggie enters, carrying cut flowers in a vase.)

MAGGIE Hello – *(She notices)*

BROWN I'll need some more paint.

MAGGIE *(horrified)* Brownie! I gave you drawing paper!

BROWN I like space. I like the big sweep – the contours of hills all flowing – don't paint leaves, I make you see trees in clumps of green.

MAGGIE Matron will have a fit.

BROWN What are the flowers?

MAGGIE You don't deserve them.

BROWN Who are they from?

MAGGIE Me.

BROWN Maggie!

MAGGIE I didn't buy them.

BROWN Pinched them?

MAGGIE Picked them.

BROWN A lovely thought. Put them over there. I should bring *you* flowers. MAGGIE I'm not ill.

BROWN Nor am I. Do you like it?

---

4 **pastoral** [ˈpɑːstərəl] having to do with country life – 4 **competent** [ˈkɒmpɪtənt] adequate, satisfactory – 4 **amateurish** [ˌæməˈtɜːrɪʃ] – 9 **big sweep** long, strong strokes with the brush – 9 **contour** [ˈkɒntʊə] outline or shape of s.th. – 11 **clump** *here:* large mass of paint – 12 **to have a fit** to have a nervous breakdown – 19 **to pinch** *(coll.)* to steal

MAGGIE Very pretty.

BROWN I'm only doing it to please matron really. I could do with a bigger brush. There's more paint, is there? I'll need a lot of blue. It's going to be summer in here.

5 MAGGIE It's summer outside. Isn't that good enough for you?

(Brown stares out of the window: gardens, flowers, trees, hills.)

BROWN I couldn't stay out there. You don't get the benefits.

MAGGIE *(leaving)* I'll have to tell matron, you know.

BROWN You don't get the looking after. And the privacy. *(He*
10 *considers.)* I'll have to take the curtains down.

---

7 **benefit** [ˈbenɪfɪt] advantage

Scene 11

(The hospital office.)

MATRON It's not as if he was psychotic.

DOCTOR Or Picasso.

MATRON What did the psychiatrist think?

DOCTOR He likes it.

MATRON About him.

DOCTOR He likes him too.

MATRON *(sour)* He's likeable.

DOCTOR He knows what he's doing.

MATRON Hiding.

DOCTOR From what? … *(Thoughtfully)* I just thought I'd let him stay the night. I wanted to go back to bed and it seemed the easiest thing to do. I thought that in the morning … Well, I'm not sure what I thought would happen in the morning.

MATRON He's not simple – he's giving nothing away. Not even to nurse Coates.

DOCTOR Well, keep her at it.

MATRON She doesn't need much keeping.

---

9 **sour** [saʊə] bad-tempered

Scene 12

(Brown's ward. Brown has painted a whole wall and is working on a second one. Maggie sits on the bed.)

MAGGIE That was when I started nursing, after that.

BROWN Funny. I would have thought your childhood was all to do with ponies and big stone-floored kitchens …

MAGGIE Goes to show. What was your childhood like?

BROWN Young … I wish I had more money.

MAGGIE You've got a lot. You must have had a good job …?

BROWN Centre-forward for Arsenal.

MAGGIE You're not fair! You don't give me anything in return.

BROWN This painting's for you, Maggie… If I'd got four times as much money, I'd take four rooms and paint one for each season. But I've only got money for the summer.

MAGGIE What will you do when it's gone?

BROWN *(seriously)* I don't know. Perhaps I'll get ill and have to go to hospital. But I'll miss you, Maggie.

MAGGIE If you had someone to look after you you wouldn't have this trouble.

BROWN What trouble?

MAGGIE If you had someone to cook your meals and do your laundry you'd be all right, wouldn't you?

BROWN It's the things that go with it.

MAGGIE You should have got married. I bet you had chances.

---

7 **goes to show** *here:* it shows that one can be mistaken in s.o. – 10 **centre-forward** *(Mittelstürmer)* – 10 **Arsenal** ['ɑːsənl] traditional London football-club

BROWN Perhaps.

MAGGIE It's not too late.

BROWN You don't think so?

MAGGIE You're attractive.

BROWN *(pause)* What are you like when you're not wearing your uniform? MAGGIE *(saucy)* Mr Brown!

BROWN *(innocent, angry)* I didn't mean –!

MAGGIE *(regretful)* Oh, I'm sorry …

BROWN *(calm)* I can't think of you not being a nurse. It belongs to another world I'm not part of any more.

MAGGIE What have you got about hospitals?

BROWN A hospital is a very dependable place. Anything could be going on outside. Since I've been in here – there could be a war on, and for once it's got nothing to do with me. I don't even know about it. Fire, flood and misery of all kinds, across the world or over the hill, it can all go on, but this is a private ward; I'm paying for it. *(Pause)* There's one thing that's always impressed me about hospitals – they've all got their own generators. In case of power cuts. And water tanks. I mean, a hospital can carry on, set loose from the world. The meals come in on trays, on the dot – the dust never settles before it's wiped – clean laundry at the appointed time – the matron does her round and temperatures are taken; pulses too, taken in pure conditions, not affected by anything outside. You need never know anything, it doesn't touch you.

MAGGIE That's not true, Brownie.

BROWN I know it's not.

---

6 **saucy** ['sɔːsɪ] cheeky, coquettish – 12 **dependable** [dɪˈpendəbl] that can be trusted – 19 **power cut** a breakdown of the electricity system – 21 **on the dot** at the proper time – 22 **appointed** fixed

MAGGIE Then you shouldn't try and make it true.

BROWN I know I shouldn't.

(Pause)

MAGGIE Is that all there is to it, then?

5 BROWN You've still got theories?

MAGGIE There's a new one. You're a retired forger.

BROWN Ha! The money's real enough.

MAGGIE I know.

BROWN How do you know?

10 MAGGIE *(shamefaced)* They had it checked.

(Brown laughs.)

BROWN They've got to make it difficult. I've got to be a crook or a lunatic.

MAGGIE Then why don't you tell them where you came from?

15 BROWN They want to pass me on. But they don't know who to, or where. I'm happy here.

MAGGIE Haven't you been happy anywhere else?

BROWN Yes. I had a good four years of it once.

MAGGIE In hospital?

20 BROWN No, that was abroad.

MAGGIE Where have you been?

BROWN All over. I've been among French, Germans, Greeks, Turks, Arabs …

---

4 **Is that all there is to it?** is there nothing more behind it? – 6 **retired** having stopped working, usually because of old age – 6 **forger** person who illegally prints banknotes – 10 **shamefaced** *here:* ashamed – 12 **crook** [krʊk] criminal – 13 **lunatic** [ˈluːnətɪk] mad person

MAGGIE What were you doing?

BROWN Different things in different places. *(Smiles)* I was painting in France.

MAGGIE An artist?

5 BROWN Oh very. Green and brown. I could turn a row of tanks into a leafy hedgerow. Not literally. Worse luck.

---

5 **tank** heavy fighting vehicle *(Panzer)* – 6 **leafy** covered with leaves – 6 **hedgerow** ['hedʒrəʊ] row of bushes – 6 **literally** *here:* really – 6 **Worse luck**. too bad

Scene 13

(The hospital office. The doctor is on the phone.)

DOCTOR … He meant camouflage … Well, I realise that, but there are a number of points to narrow the field … His age, for one thing. I know they were all the same age … Must be records of some kind .. Service in France and Germany, probably Cyprus, Middle East – Aden possibly …

---

3 **camouflage** [ˈkæməflɑːʒ] the use of paint etc. to hide military vehicles – 4 **to narrow the field** to limit the range of possibilities

Scene 14

(Brown's ward. Brown has painted two walls and is working on a third.)

MAGGIE It's very nice, Brownie. Perhaps you'll be famous and people will come here to see your mural.

BROWN I wouldn't let them in.

MAGGIE After you're dead. In a hundred years.

BROWN Yes, they could come in then.

MAGGIE What will you do when you've finished the room?

BROWN Go back to bed and pick up the threads of my old life. It'll be nice in here. Hospital routine in a pastoral setting. That's kind of perfection, really.

MAGGIE You could have put your bed in the garden.

BROWN What's the date?

MAGGIE The 27th.

BROWN I've lasted well, haven't I?

MAGGIE How old are you?

BROWN Twice your age.

MAGGIE Forty-four?

BROWN And more. *(Looking close)* What are you thinking?

MAGGIE Only thinking.

BROWN Yes?

MAGGIE Before I was born, you were in the war.

---

5 **mural** ['mjʊərəl] a wall-painting – 10 **to pick up the threads of one's old life** [θred] to take up one's old life again

BROWN *(moves)* Yes. Private Brown.

MAGGIE Was it awful being in the war?

BROWN I didn't like the first bit. But in the end it was very nice.

MAGGIE What happened to you?

BROWN I got taken prisoner.

MAGGIE Oh. Well, you're still private, aren't you, Brownie?

BROWN Better than being dead.

MAGGIE Being private?

BROWN A prisoner … Four years.

MAGGIE Is that where you were happy?

BROWN Yes … Funny thing, that camp. Up to then it was all terrible. Chaos – all the pins must have fallen off the map. The queue on the beach – dive bombers and bullets. Oh dear, yes. The camp was like breathing out for the first time in months. I couldn't believe it. It was like winning, being captured. Well, it gets different people in different ways. Some couldn't stand it and some went by the book – yes, it's a duty to escape. They were digging like ferrets. They had a hole out of my hut right into the pines. There were twenty in the hut and I watched all nineteen of them go off.
They were all back in a week except one who was dead. I didn't care what they called me, I'd won. The war was still going on but I wasn't going to it any more. They gave us food, life was regulated, in a box of earth and wire and sky, and sometimes you'd hear an aeroplane miles up, but it

---

1 **private** ordinary soldier without rank – 14 **dive bomber** [ˈdaɪvbɒmə] aircraft dropping bombs while diving steeply towards a target – 14 **bullet** [ˈbʊlɪt] piece of metal fired from a gun – 17 **captured** [ˈkæptʃəd] taken prisoner – 18 **to go by the book** to stick to the rules – 19 **ferret** [ˈferɪt] small animal like a weasel (*Frettchen*) – 20 **pine** *(Kiefer, Pinie)*

couldn't touch you. On my second day I knew what it reminded me of.

MAGGIE What?

BROWN Here. It reminded me of here.

Scene 15

(The hospital office. Present are the doctor, matron and Maggie. The doctor is holding a big book – a ledger of admissions, his finger on a line.)

DOCTOR John Brown. And an address. *(Looks up)* It was obvious. *(To Maggie)* Well done.

MAGGIE *(troubled)* But does it make any difference?

MATRON What was he doing round here?

DOCTOR Staying with relatives – or holiday, we can find out.

MAGGIE So long ago?

DOCTOR Compound fracture – car accident. The driver paid for him Well, something to go on at last!

MAGGIE But he hasn't done anything wrong, has he?

---

3 **ledger of admissions** [ˈledʒə] book in which all admissions are recorded –
11 **compound fracture** [ˌkɒmpaʊndˈfræktʃə] breaking of a bone complicated by an open wound

Scene 16

(Brown's ward. The painting nearly covers the walls. Brown is finishing it off in one corner.)

BROWN I was a Regular, you see, and peace didn't match up to the war I'd had. There was too much going on.

MAGGIE So what did you do then?

BROWN This and that. Didn't fancy a lot. I thought I'd like to be a lighthouse keeper but it didn't work out. Didn't like the company.

MAGGIE Company?

BROWN There were three of us.

MAGGIE Oh.

BROWN Then I thought I'd be a sort of monk, but they wouldn't have me because I didn't believe, didn't believe enough for their purposes. I asked them to let me stay without being a proper monk but they weren't having any of that. . . . What I need is a sort of monastery for agnostics.

MAGGIE Like a hospital for the healthy.

BROWN That's it.

MAGGIE *(exasperated)* Brownie!

(He paints.)

BROWN Shouldn't you be working, or something?

MAGGIE I'll go if you like.

---

4 **Regular** soldier of the regular army (as opposed to guerillas) – 4 **to match up to** to be equal to – 7 **to fancy** to have a liking for – 17 **they weren't having any of that** they didn't accept that – 18 **monastery** [ˈmɒnəstrɪ] house in which monks live – 18 **agnostic** [æɡˈnɒstɪk] one who believes that nothing can be known about God – 21 **exasperated** [ɪɡˈzɑːspəreɪtɪd] angry, irritated

BROWN I like you being here. Just wondered.

MAGGIE Wondered what?

BROWN I'm telling you about myself, aren't I? I shouldn't put you in that position – if they find out they'll blame you for not passing it on.

MAGGIE But you haven't done anything wrong, have you, Brownie?

BROWN Is that what you're here for?

MAGGIE No.

(Brown finishes off the painting and stands back.)

BROWN There.

MAGGIE It's lovely.

BROWN Yes. Quite good. It'll be nice, to sit here inside my painting. I'll enjoy that.

---

5 **to pass s.th. on** to give information to s.o. else

Scene 17

(The hospital office. The doctor is on the phone.)

DOCTOR … Brown. John Brown – yes, he was here before, a long time ago – we've got him in the records – Mmm – and an address. We'll start checking … there must be *somebody* …

---

4 **in the records** on the list of names

Scene 18

(Brown's ward. The walls are covered with paintings. Brown is sitting on the bed. The door opens and a strange nurse – nurse Jones – enters with Brown's lunch on a tray.)

JONES Are you ready for lunch –?

(Sees the painting)

My, my, aren't you clever – it's better than anyone would have thought.

BROWN Where's Maggie?

JONES NURSE Coates? I don't know.

BROWN But – she's my nurse.

JONES Yours? Well, she's everybody's.

BROWN *(worried)* You don't understand – she's looking after me, you see.

(The doctor enters; nurse Jones leaves.)

DOCTOR *(cheerful)* Well, Mr BROWN – good news!

BROWN *(wary)* Yes?

DOCTOR You're going to have visitors.

BROWN Visitors?

DOCTOR Your sister Mabel and her husband. They were amazed to hear from you.

BROWN They didn't hear from *me*.

DOCTOR They're travelling up tomorrow. All your friends had been wondering where you'd got to –

BROWN *(getting more peevish)* What friends?

25 **peevish** bad-tempered

DOCTOR Well, there's an old army friend, isn't there – what's his name –?

BROWN I don't know. Where's nurse Coates gone?

DOCTOR Nowhere. She's round about. I think she's on nights downstairs this week. I understand that you were here once before – as a child.

BROWN Yes.

DOCTOR You are a dark horse, aren't you? To tell you quite frankly, we did wonder about you – some quite romantic ideas, not entirely creditable either –

BROWN I told you – I told you there was nothing like that – Why couldn't you –?

DOCTOR Your brother-in-law said something about a job, thought you might be interested.

BROWN *(angrily)* You couldn't leave well alone, could you?

DOCTOR *(pause; not phoney any more)* It's not enough, Mr Brown. You've got to … *connect* …

---

4 **on nights** on night duty – 8 **a dark horse** person who does s.th. clever or successful when no one expected him to do so – 10 **creditable** ['krɛdɪtəbl] favourable – 16 **phoney** ['fəʊnɪ] insincere

Scene 19

(The hospital office. Brown appears, dressed, carrying his bags, from the direction of his room. He sees Maggie and stops. She sees him.)

MAGGIE Brownie! Where are you going?

BROWN Back.

MAGGIE Back where?

(He does not answer.)

You've got nothing to run for, have you. Nothing to hide. I *know* you haven't.

BROWN I know you know. They've been busy … I wasn't worth the trouble, you know.

MAGGIE You blame me.

BROWN No. No, I don't, *really*. You had to tell them, didn't you?

MAGGIE I'm sorry – I –

BROWN You thought it was for the best.

MAGGIE Yes, I did. I still do. It's not good for you, what you're doing.

BROWN How do you know? – *you* mean it wouldn't be good for *you*. How do you know what's good for me?

MAGGIE They're coming tomorrow. Family, friends; isn't that good?

BROWN I could have found them, if I'd wanted. I didn't come here for that. *(Comes up to her)* They won. *(Looks out through frontdoors)* I feel I should breathe in before going out there.

MAGGIE I can't let you go, Brownie.

BROWN *(gently mocking)* Regulations?

MAGGIE I can't.

BROWN I'm free to come and go. I'm paying.

MAGGIE I know – but it is a hospital.

BROWN *(smiles briefly)* I'm not ill. Don't wake the doctor, he doesn't like being woken. *(Moves)* Don't be sorry – I had a good time here with you. Do you think they'll leave my painting?

MAGGIE Brownie …

BROWN Trouble is, I've always been so *well*. If I'd been *sick* I would have been all right.

(He goes out into the night.)

---

1 **to mock s.o.** to tease, to make fun of s.o.

Biographical Notes

Tom Stoppard was born on July 3, 1937 in Czechoslovakia, the son of Eugene Straussler. In 1939 his family moved to Singapore. Before the Japanese invasion in 1942 the family was evacuated to India and his father, who remained behind, was killed. His mother married Kenneth Stoppard, a soldier in the British Army in India. From 1954 to 1960 Tom Stoppard was employed by British papers as a news reporter and theatre and film critic. In 1960 he finished his first play, *A Walk on the Water*, later re-titled *Enter a Free Man*. During the following years he was a free-lance journalist and drama critic. He was commissioned to write short plays and episodes for radio serials. After the broadcast of several of his plays on TV, including *A Separate Peace*, which was televised in 1966, his first world-wide success was the production of *Rosencrantz and Guildenstern are Dead* (1967), a comedy about Hamlet's friends who find themselves in the situation of having the commission to spy on Hamlet and take him to England without knowing at all what is really going on at the Danish Court.

To the present day Stoppard has written a considerable number of plays, among which the most important are *Jumpers* (1972), *Travesties* (1974), *Night and Day* (1978), *The Real Thing* (1982), *Arcadia* (1993), *The Invention of Love* (1997) and *The Coast of Utopia* (2002). Stoppard's plays combine serious topics with comedy. Grotesque situations are sometimes presented through a fireworks of verbal wit. Stoppard has also written several radio plays and film scripts, among them the award-winning *Shakespeare in Love* (1998). He himself confesses to having been influenced by the comedies of Oscar Wilde. Stoppard is widely considered the leading contemporary British comedy writer. In 2008 he was awarded 'The Critics' Circle Award for Distinguished Service to the Arts'.

James Saunders
A Slight Accident

There is the sound of a shot. As the curtain rises Penelope is standing, becomingly, with an equivocal expression on her face and a revolver, still smoking, in her hand. At some distance lies the body of a man. Penelope, looking perhaps rather as might a woman of means who had just broken her husband's favourite piece of antique china, looks at the body, without moving towards it, then at the revolver. It continues to smoke. She waves it about, blows down the barrel, coughs, fans away gracefully the trace of gun-smoke still hanging in the air, and considers the situation.

PENELOPE   Oh dear … *(She goes up to the body, peers at it without stooping.)* Harry … Harry dear, don't be ridiculous … really, if you can't take a joke … Will you please get up … Harry, do get up … Harry! Harry? *(She gently nudges it with her toe.)* Harry?

(No answer. She goes to the telephone, dials, and waits.)

Hallo, Camilla darling. Am I disturbing you? … You are? Oh … I wondered if you could come up for a few minutes … No, I can't wait. I've just done something rather tiresome and I need company. Come and watch the rest of the – My husband isn't much company at the moment … You don't know at all what I mean … Darling, please … Yes, we've had it fixed … Yes, the picture's perfect now … That's sweet of you.

---

2 **becomingly** in a graceful manner – 2 **equivocal** [ɪˈkwɪvəkl] mysterious – 5 **a woman of means** a rich woman – 8 **barrel** the metal tube of a revolver – 8 **to fan** to wave one's hand or some object to produce a current of air – 11 **to peer** to look closely – 12 **to stoop** to bend the body forwards and downwards – 14 **to nudge** to touch slightly – 19 **tiresome** *here:* likely to cause some trouble – 22 **to have s. th. fixed** *here:* to have s. th. repaired

(She hangs up, switches on the television, looks at the body again.)

Everything happens to me …

(She takes another look at the body, goes to the door, turns back as though coming in for the first time.)

Penelope darling – Oh …

(She hurriedly covers the body with a bearskin rug. She arranges meticulously and with taste several cushions on the rug. The doorbell rings. She goes to answer it. The television comes on as she comes back with Camilla.)

CAMILLA Penelope darling, what *has* happened?

(Penelope says nothing. Her eyes on Penelope, Camilla sits before the television, and is drawn into it. Penelope walks to and fro, rehearsing her lines.)

ACTRESS 1 I've had this to say for twenty years: you're rotten, you've always been rotten and you always will be rotten.

ACTRESS 2 You despise me …

ACTRESS 1 You killed my brother. You drove my son to suicide. You ruined my cousin. All you touch you defile.

(Sobs)

ACTRESS 1 You sent my husband mad; you corrupted his nephew.

ACTRESS 2 Why do you hate me?

(Sobs. Sound of door opening)

ACTRESS 1 You're filthy. Filthy.

7 **bearskin rug** the skin of a bear, used as a carpet – 8 **meticulously** [mɪˈtɪkjʊləslɪ] carefully – 14 **to and fro** backwards and forwards – 14 **to rehearse** to practise a play, piece of music, etc. – 15 **rotten** *here*: disagreeable, very unpleasant – 19 **to drive s.o. to suicide** [ˈsjuːɪsaɪd] to make s.o. kill himself – 19 **to defile**[dɪˈfaɪl] to make dirty – 25 **filthy** dirty, disgusting

ACTRESS 2 Philip! Thank God you're safe.

(Sound of door closing)

ACTOR 1 My God I need a drink.

(Sound of door opening)

ACTRESS 1 I'm going to my room.

(Sound of door closing)

ACTRESS 2 Philip, where's …?

ACTOR 1 Dead.

(Sound of breath being caught)

ACTRESS 2 How …?

ACTOR 1 Tincture of iodine. Evelyn can't we start afresh? Go away somewhere?

ACTRESS 2 Where?

ACTOR 1 Anywhere. Trucial Oman.

ACTRESS 2 You mean – Together? You're vile. Vile …

ACTOR 1 You fool. Don't you realise this is your last chance?

ACTRESS 2 I can't take any more, I can't, I can't!!!

(Sobs. Sound of door opening)

ACTRESS 1 I heard a shot.

ACTOR 1 What!

ACTRESS 2 Not …

(Sound of door opening. Sound of doorbell)

---

11 **tincture of iodine** [ˈtɪŋktʃərəvˈaɪədiːn] liquid for disinfecting wounds *(Jod)* – 11 **afresh** again – 14 **Trucial Oman** [ˈtruːsjəl əʊˈmɑːn] country in Arabia – 15 **vile** [vaɪl] disgusting

Oh God … Vincent!

(Sound of door closing)

ACTOR 2 Quite a pretty picture, isn't it? Well, the time has come.

5 ACTOR 1 My God I need a drink.

(Sound of telephone)

ACTRESS 1 Don't answer it! It's a trap!

(Sound of door closing. Sound of doorbell)

ACTRESS 2 Look out, he's got a knife!

10 ACTOR 2 You've had your last drink, you swine!

(Sound of a shot. Sound of breath being caught. Sound of gurgling. Silence. Sound of a glassful of whisky and soda dripping onto a tiled fireplace. Silence. Sound of a body dropping onto the floor.)

15 ACTRESS 2 He's …

ACTOR 1 Dead.

ACTRESS 2 You'd better go.

ACTRESS 1 And leave you …?

ACTRESS 2 Yes. Leave me. Go.

20 *(Sound of door closing)*

ACTOR 1 Coming, Claire?

(Sound of door opening)

ACTOR 2 You'll be all right?

(Sound of door closing)

---

12 **to gurgle** to make a bubbling sound

ACTRESS 2 I'll be all right. Leave the gun.

(Sound of door closing. Silence. A shot. Silence. Sound of a body falling on to the floor. Music. Camilla looks round at Penelope, arguing with herself. She switches off.)

5 CAMILLA I'll not watch part two after all.

PENELOPE No?

CAMILLA I don't think so. All the interesting characters are dead already.

PENELOPE That's what I always say.

10 CAMILLA Where's Harry?

PENELOPE Who?

CAMILLA Your husband …

PENELOPE What about him?

CAMILLA Where is he?

15 PENELOPE Why?

CAMILLA I'm only asking.

PENELOPE Why do you ask, what do you mean, do you think I've murdered him or something, why are you looking at me like that? As a matter of fact he's lying down.

20 CAMILLA Isn't he well?

PENELOPE No. Yes. I don't know.

CAMILLA You must know.

PENELOPE Why must I?

CAMILLA But darling -

---

4 **to argue** to debate

PENELOPE I don't live in my husband's pocket. Harry's a free agent; if he wants to be well or unwell he doesn't have to give me an account of it. Do you think I go running around after Harry saying, are you well, Harry, are you still well?

CAMILLA Forget I asked …

PENELOPE He wanted to lie down, so he lay down.

CAMILLA All right, darling.

(Pause)

So what's the trouble?

(Penelope looks at her.)

You said you'd done something stupid.

PENELOPE I didn't say that at all. I don't know what you mean.

CAMILLA Penelope darling, you rang me up -

PENELOPE I didn't say stupid.

CAMILLA Let's not play with words …

PENELOPE Why not, words are important. What do we have to play with but words? I'm not going to have you coming up here at a moment's notice accusing me of being stupid.

CAMILLA Oh, dear …

PENELOPE What I said was 'tiresome'. It was an accident.

CAMILLA What was?

PENELOPE To be stupid you have to do it on purpose. It's like breaking the handle off a cup; if you do it on purpose that's stupid but if it's an accident it's tiresome, that's all, certainly not stupid. I didn't do it on purpose … don't think…

---

2 **a free agent** s.o. who can choose freely how to act – 3 **account** report

CAMILLA You didn't.

PENELOPE Why should I?

CAMILLA But why all this fuss about breaking a handle off a cup?

PENELOPE I haven't broken any handles, darling, it's nothing to do with handles.

CAMILLA I see.

PENELOPE You don't see.

CAMILLA Very true.

(Pause)

Are you going to give me a drink?

(Penelope begins to go through the usual motions.)

I do like your curtains … Of course, you don't have to tell me anything …

PENELOPE Give me time, darling … Some things are so silly they're embarrassing. I mean, there's the normal course of events carrying itself along as usual, in a nice straight grey line, and then suddenly out of the blue there's this ludicrous occurrence, spoiling the whole natural sequence.
(She is still busying herself with the drinks.)
I mean, life is full of actions you couldn't possibly explain. Nearly everything we do is – inexplicable. And what difference does it make if the result of a particular action happens to be rather – extreme? … *(She turns.)* Camilla darling …

CAMILLA Penelope … What's that?

---

3 **fuss** unnecessary excitement – 12 **the usual motions** *here*: the action of preparing a drink – 18 **out of the blue** unexpectedly – 19 **ludicrous occurrence** [ˈluːdɪkrəs əˈkʌrens] ridiculous event – 20 **to busy o.s.** to make or keep o.s. busy – 22 **inexplicable** impossible to explain

PENELOPE What?

CAMILLA That heap.

PENELOPE Heap?

CAMILLA There.

PENELOPE I don't see anything.

CAMILLA It looks like a body covered with a bearskin rug, with cushions for camouflage.

PENELOPE Ridiculous.

CAMILLA May I look?

PENELOPE It's a bearskin rug, there's nothing there, I don't know what you're talking about – I forbid you to touch it! I asked you up because I thought I could rely upon you as a friend.

CAMILLA I'd like to help -

PENELOPE I took you for a woman of delicacy and understanding.

CAMILLA But I don't know what to be understanding *about*.

PENELOPE And all you can do is pry into my life and peer under my carpets as though you expect to find bodies under them all, and then you accuse me of shooting my husband.

CAMILLA Shooting your – ?

PENELOPE There you go again!

CAMILLA But I didn't mention -

---

7 **for camouflage** ['kæməflɑːʒ] in order to deceive the observer by giving a false appearance to things – 12 **to rely** upon s.o. to trust s.o. – 15 **delicacy** ['delɪkəsɪ] tact and sensitivity – 18 **to pry into s.th.** to inquire too curiously into other people's affairs

PENELOPE Then why make these grotesque allusions to a perfectly ordinary rug and a few cushions?

CAMILLA It was a joke, darling -

PENELOPE A joke! You think it's a joke!

5 CAMILLA As for your husband, I didn't mention your husband. It just looked like an anonymous body, that's all; it could be anyone's husband.

PENELOPE And I suppose you're thinking: ah, I didn't notice the shot because there were shots in the play and I mistook
10 the sound of Penelope shooting her husband for someone in the play getting shot. And now you're trying to think back to whether there was one more shot than there were bodies. You've got it all worked out, haven't you? I dare say you've decided on a motive too. Well, let me inform you that in all
15 the years of our marriage Harry and I have never once quarrelled, not once. Show me another couple you can say that about, give me their names. Harry and I have lived in perfect harmony. *There*, there are the slippers I laid out ready for him, just where he knows he can find them; there
20 is the bunch of flowers he brings me home regularly every single Thursday, for some reason. My God, I do think one could expect at least one's friends to show a little understanding and sympathy and not go leaping to the most bizarre conclusions at every opportunity. Well, it's as they
25 say: you climb in company, but you fall alone, and woe betide you if you expect your closest friend to stretch out a hand to check your descent.

CAMILLA You're not unique, you know.

PENELOPE Hm?

---

1 **allusion** indirect reference, hint – 13 **worked out** calculated in detail – 13 **I daresay** I suppose – 18 **slipper** a light shoe worn in the house – 23 **to leap** to conclusions to form a judgement too quickly – 26 **woe betide you if** may misfortune come to you if – 27 **check your descent** keep you from falling down – 28 **unique** [juːˈniːk] the only one of its kind

CAMILLA I've never quarrelled with Rodger either. Rodger's never quarrelled in his life; he doesn't believe in it. Rodger thinks one should never raise one's voice after the age of two.

PENELOPE Then you know what I'm talking about.

CAMILLA I know what you're talking about, darling.

PENELOPE Another drink?

CAMILLA Yes please … May one ask one question?

PENELOPE Hm?

CAMILLA You won't think I'm prying?

PENELOPE Probably.

CAMILLA That is a boot, is it?

PENELOPE Not at all. It's a shoe.

CAMILLA I see.

(Penelope hands her a drink.)

PENELOPE It's been one of those days, you know?

(Pause)

CAMILLA The evenings are drawing in …

PENELOPE Darling, you don't have to fill in the pauses.

(Pause)

PENELOPE Language is so limited.

CAMILLA Hm?

---

16 **one of those days** one of those days that are full of trouble – 18 **the evenings are drawing in** it is becoming dark earlier

PENELOPE Who was that scientist who was once caught, alone in his room, dropping a little bit of cotton wool into a basin, to see whether he could hear it hit the bottom?

(Camilla takes a long look at her.)

Can you imagine him trying to explain himself? Of *course* he knew he wouldn't be able to hear it. He just did it because he knew it wouldn't work … Let me start at the beginning, darling. You see, what happened –

(Door bell. Pause)

CAMILLA Shall I go?

(Penelope nods. Camilla goes; she comes back with Rodger, who is dressed as one might expect a stockbroker's son to be dressed at ten in the evening.)

RODGER I'm not following you about, dear; it's just that I'd made the cocoa –

CAMILLA I'm sorry, darling, Rodger's come up.

RODGER You don't have to apologise. How are you, Penelope?

PENELOPE Oh, I'm – first class.

RODGER Jolly good. And Harry?

PENELOPE He's first class.

RODGER Mhm. Well, dear, what are we going to do about the cocoa?

CAMILLA Do we have to do anything about it?

RODGER It's down there getting cold. *(To Penelope)* I go into the kitchen as I do every evening, make the cocoa, take it into the lounge and I find my wife's disappeared. Upset the routine completely.

---

2 **cotton wool** *(Watte)* – 12 **stockbroker** *(Börsenmakler)* – 26 **lounge** [laʊndʒ] sitting-room – 26 **to upset** to overturn, to overthrow

CAMILLA Go and drink the cocoa if you want to.

RODGER It isn't the cocoa, dear, it's the principle of the thing. Whether I drink the cocoa or not, the routine's been upset; you can't get away from it. I say, what's that?

PENELOPE Nothing.

RODGER Yes, but what is it?

PENELOPE Why is everyone so inquisitive? I invite people up and all they do is poke around asking what's this, what's that? It's an Axminster carpet wrapped up in a bearskin rug.

RODGER But –

PENELOPE The cleaners are calling for it in the morning – the carpet, the rug and the cushions. They all need cleaning.

RODGER Yes, but –

PENELOPE Down the centre of the carpet is a long pole to make it easier to carry the carpet and on the end of the pole is a shoe, so that the person carrying the carpet will not be injured by the end of the pole. The shoe is a safety measure. Now I hope everyone's satisfied.

RODGER There seem to be two shoes.

PENELOPE Then there must be two poles, mustn't there? What will you drink?

RODGER Cocoa. Where's Harry?

PENELOPE Whisky or gin?

RODGER Yes, please. Where's – ?

PENELOPE *(pouring a drink)* He's out of town.

---

7 inquisitive [ɪnˈkwɪzətɪv] eager to learn details about other people's affairs – **8 to poke around** *(coll.)* to search around – **9 Axminster carpet** type of carpet, called after its place of origin – **11 to call for s.th.** to come and fetch s.th. – **14 pole** a stick – **17 measure** action taken *(Maßnahme)*

RODGER Out of town?

PENELOPE Yes.

RODGER I thought he was in town.

PENELOPE He was in town, now he's out of town.

CAMILLA Not lying down.

RODGER Out of town not lying down?

PENELOPE He's out of town lying down. Is there anything to prevent that?

CAMILLA If he's out of town how do you know he's lying down?

PENELOPE He rang me up.

CAMILLA To say he was lying down.

PENELOPE *Yes.* He rang me up to say he was out of town, and that he was lying down. He was lying down when he rang me up. Do you mind?

CAMILLA Lying down in a telephone box.

PENELOPE No, darling, in a hotel bedroom. He rang me from an out-of-town bedside telephone to say he was lying down.

(Pause)

RODGER Is Harry in the habit of – ?

PENELOPE Why are you persecuting me?

CAMILLA It just seems a little unusual …

PENELOPE What are you insinuating? That he isn't out of town lying down? That he's in town standing up? Is that what you're getting at?

---

21 **to persecute s.o.** ['pɜːsɪkjuːt] to trouble s.o. continually – 23 **to insinuate s.th.** [ɪn'sɪnjʊeɪt] to suggest s.th. indirectly and unpleasantly

CAMILLA No, darling …

PENELOPE Do you think I have him standing up in a cupboard somewhere? Do you? Do you want to search my cupboards? Really, this is too bad.

(Pause)

RODGER Leeds?

CAMILLA What?

RODGER I was talking to Penelope.

PENELOPE What?

RODGER Leeds?

PENELOPE Leads what?

RODGER The town Leeds.

PENELOPE The town leads what?

RODGER Is it the town Leeds?

PENELOPE Is what the town Leeds?

RODGER Is Harry in the town Leeds?

PENELOPE No.

RODGER He was last year.

PENELOPE Well he isn't this year.

(Pause)

CAMILLA Where then?

PENELOPE Oh … Hull.

(Pause)

CAMILLA Why go to Hull to lie down?

PENELOPE I don't want to pursue this subject.

CAMILLA All right, darling.

(Pause)

RODGER Why not?

PENELOPE I just don't.

RODGER Mhm.

PENELOPE He had to go to Hull to see a client.

CAMILLA In a hotel.

PENELOPE In an office, in an office.

RODGER Then they went to the hotel –

PENELOPE Then *he* went to the hotel, since he felt unwell, and lay on the bed and rang me up. Do you want his telephone number as well!

RODGER I could give him a ring –

PENELOPE Well you're not going to. I'm not going to have him pestered by all and sundry when he's not well … Poor Harry …

RODGER Poor old Harry … It's his own fault, of course.

PENELOPE What do you mean?

RODGER Breaking his routine. It leads to trouble. He goes to Hull, a thing he never does; he becomes ill. Naturally. He should have let the client come to London. Let the client be sick.

CAMILLA What are you talking about?

RODGER Look at me. Am I ever ill? No. Why?

---

1 **to pursue a subject** [pəˈsjuː] to go on talking about a subject – 16 **to pester s.o.** to annoy s.o. continually – 16 **all and sundry** everybody

CAMILLA Because you haven't the imagination.

RODGER Because I stick to routine. Because I have every action catalogued, right down to the blowing of my nose at set intervals.

5 PENELOPE Catalogued?

RODGER I keep a book. A sort of manual of running instructions. I've worked it out over the years. What's childhood for if not to learn one's running routine? By the time I was twenty I knew precisely what I'd be doing any
10 minute of the day. It's the only way to live safely. Behind the facade, no, the bastion of habit, of routine, anarchy lurks, waiting to spring …

CAMILLA Rodger dear –

RODGER Look at this case in the paper today. A hairdresser's
15 assistant in Balham is working quietly along a row of seven ladies sitting under the hairdriers when suddenly he takes up a pair of scissors and stabs all seven of them one after another. Why did it happen? I'll tell you: he lost respect for routine, he threw his habits over-board. He left the well-
20 ordered terrain of habituality and struck off into the jungle of infinite possibility, where every step is into unknown country. Think of him. I may continue to dry the hair of these women who mean nothing to me, he says to himself. I may go along the line asking are they comfortable and
25 offering them the *Tatler* and *Country Life*; but equally I may not. But if not, what? Indeed, what not?

(Pause)

---

1 **imagination** power of the mind to imagine s.th. – 3 **to catalogue** [ˈkætəlɒg] to put in a list – 4 **at set intervals** regularly, at fixed times – 7 **a manual of running instructions** *here:* a handbook on how to run one's daily life – 11 **facade** [fəˈsɑːd] the front of a building, also: false appearance – 11 **to lurk** to lie in wait and ready to attack – 17 **to stab** to wound or kill with a pointed instrument – 20 **to strike off** to go off – 21 **infinite** [ˈɪnfɪnɪt] endless, unlimited – 25 **Tatler, Country Life** *(names of two magazines)*

CAMILLA What are you trying to prove?

RODGER That I'm invulnerable; impregnable; safe.

CAMILLA That you'll never stab a woman with a pair of scissors while she's sitting under a hairdrier.

5 RODGER Yes, for instance. Tell me, have I ever committed a crime? Ever run anyone over or been run over? Ever missed a train? I'm a creature of habit; I'm as safe as houses.

PENELOPE You shouldn't be too sure.

RODGER Well, here's the proof.

10 PENELOPE Where?

RODGER Here. Me. I sit here after thirty-nine years without a scar, without a worry, without a stain on my character; I did today what I did yesterday, and I shall do tomorrow what I did today. Nothing went wrong today, nothing can go wrong
15 tomorrow. If I meet the untoward on my way, I shall size it up from a distance, and walk gingerly round it.

CAMILLA What have you got there, Rodger?

(Rodger, in making himself more comfortable in his chair, has removed' the hard lump from under his cushion. He stares at
20 *it.)*

PENELOPE Be careful, Rodger, it may have a hair-trigger.

RODGER It's not loaded, obviously.

PENELOPE D'you want to try it?

---

2 **invulnerable** that cannot be wounded or hurt - **impregnable** that resists all attacks – 6 **to run s.o. over** to pass over s.o. in a vehicle – 7 **as safe as houses** very safe – 12 **scar** mark remaining on skin as the result of a wound – 12 **stain** dirty mark – 15 **to meet the untoward** [ˌʌntəˈwɔːd] to meet s.th. unfavourable or inconvenient – 16 **to size s.th. up** to form a judgement or opinion of s.th. – 16 **gingerly** [ˈdʒɪndʒəlɪ] with great care and caution to avoid harming oneself – 19 **lump** a solid mass of material – 21 **hair-trigger** small tongue of metal which fires a gun or revolver at the slightest pressure

(Rodger examines it.)

CAMILLA Loaded? *(He nods.)*

PENELOPE You see?

RODGER Isn't it rather dangerous, leaving loaded revolvers lying around?

PENELOPE It isn't leaving them lying around that's dangerous, it's picking them up and pulling the trigger. There you are, you see, the man of habit, sitting drinking gin and tonic with a loaded revolver pointed at your wife.

RODGER The safety catch is on; I do know a little about revolvers.

PENELOPE Do you know how little one finger has to move in order to pull the trigger?

RODGER I tell you the safety catch is on.

PENELOPE Do you know how little the thumb has to move to put it off?

(Rodger smells the barrel.)

RODGER It's been fired.

PENELOPE Has it?

RODGER One shot.

PENELOPE Really?

RODGER Recently.

(Pause)

PENELOPE Yes. That's right. It was me.

RODGER You?

---

14 **safety catch** a device which prevents a gun from being fired by accident

PENELOPE Yes. I pulled the trigger.

CAMILLA When?

PENELOPE This evening. I had it in my hand and the trigger got pulled.

RODGER By you.

PENELOPE Who else?

CAMILLA So there *was* an extra shot.

RODGER During the play. Of course. There was a shot, and no one fell down. It seemed rather strange at the time.

PENELOPE That's what it was, you see.

CAMILLA What were you firing at? Or was it an accident?

PENELOPE More drinks, anyone?

RODGER Of course it was an accident, what else could it have been?

PENELOPE More drinks?

CAMILLA Was it?

PENELOPE What?

CAMILLA An accident?

PENELOPE Now let's see, yours was a gin as well, wasn't it? … Yes, of course it was an accident.

CAMILLA You just picked it up and it went off.

PENELOPE I just picked it up and – pulled the trigger.

RODGER By accident.

PENELOPE Naturally … That is to say …

CAMILLA What?

PENELOPE That is to say, I pulled the *trigger* on purpose. If that's what you mean.

CAMILLA What else could we mean, darling?

RODGER So it *wasn't* an accident.

PENELOPE It *was*.

CAMILLA But you did it deliberately.

PENELOPE I didn't do it deliberately ... I did it on purpose ...

CAMILLA *Darling* ...

PENELOPE Oh, *really* ... Why are you so *obtuse*? Why do you pretend everything's so *simple*?

CAMILLA There's accident, darling, and there's design, darling – –

PENELOPE And there's Rodger sitting there with a glass in his hand, about to raise it to his lips.

RODGER I don't get the drift.

PENELOPE Did you pick it up deliberately?

RODGER Yes ... Well – half deliberately ...

PENELOPE *Half* deliberately; *Rodger* ... You picked it up, on purpose to drink it, without deliberation ... You raise it to your lips, and take a sip, on purpose to drink it, without deliberation. And if the glass contained poison, and by some accident nothing happened to stop you –

RODGER But it doesn't.

PENELOPE Or if it were not a glass of gin and tonic but a revolver, and you didn't raise it to your lips without

---

6 **deliberately** after thinking about it, on purpose – 9 **obtuse** [əbˈtjuːs] slow in understanding – 11 **design** *here:* purpose – 15 **I don't get the drift** I don't get the meaning – 19 **deliberation** careful consideration – 20 **to take a sip** to drink just a few drops

deliberation but raised it with your finger on the trigger, without deliberation, and somebody said 'Pull it' and you pulled …

RODGER   I don't know what you're talking about.

PENELOPE   I picked up the revolver, just as you picked up that glass; I put my finger on the trigger, as one does automatically; I held it up like this, as one does; and …

RODGER   You *pulled* the *trigger*.

PENELOPE   And by some - accident, by some mischance … nothing happened to stop me …

(Slight pause)

PENELOPE   Of all the thousand and one things that could have happened, nothing did … Suppose, for instance, there'd been a mouse.

RODGER   A mouse?

PENELOPE   *A mouse*, yes …

RODGER   You shot at a mouse?

PENELOPE   No, Rodger, I didn't shoot at a mouse, but let's say there *was* a mouse; which ran out from under that chair.

RODGER   Impossible.

PENELOPE   What's impossible about it?

RODGER   There are no mice.

PENELOPE   How do you know? How do you know what's behind the wainscot?

RODGER   If there were mice in this flat, there'd be mice in our flat.

---

9 mischance [ˌmɪsˈtʃɑːns] bad luck – **24 wainscot** wooden panelling on the lower half of the walls

PENELOPE We could have our own private mice, couldn't we?

RODGER No, because they'd have to pass our flat to get here.

PENELOPE Well they did. They came during the day, while you were out. Or watching television. There were mice on television and you thought you were hearing television mice scuttling by, just as with the shot. My finger was on the trigger, when suddenly – out from under that chair, frightened by a cat, ran the mouse.

RODGER Cat! What cat?

PENELOPE A cat, any cat. A cat from downstairs. It came up, attracted by the smell of milk.

RODGER There's no cat downstairs. We have no cat; the Fergusons on the first floor, they have no cat; the Hartleys on the ground floor, they have no cat. Even the porter has no cat. Then whose cat was it?

PENELOPE It was *no one's* cat. It was a stray cat. The town's full of stray cats, wild cats, cats that have never known a proper home. Born in coal cellars and, and bicycle sheds, fending for themselves. It's the old story. They eat what they can; it's a hard life. This one was looking for mice on the stairs.

CAMILLA You said it smelt milk.

PENELOPE It smelt milk and forgot the mice. But when it got up here it smelt mice and forgot the milk. The cat crept behind the chair and the mouse, which had been attracted by the smell of the biscuits I was to have with my milk –

CAMILLA You don't drink milk, Penelope …

PENELOPE Camilla, *please* … The mouse, alarmed, bounded from under the chair –

---

6 **to scuttle by** to run quickly and anxiously – 14 **porter** doorman – 16 **a stray cat** a cat without a home – 19 **to fend for o.s.** to look after o.s. – 27 **to bound** to jump

RODGER Followed by the cat.

PENELOPE Followed by the cat, and I, surprised, forgot that I'd been about to accidentally, on purpose, without deliberation, pull the trigger, and … didn't. That would have been an accident, wouldn't it? So, by the same token, it was an accident that, as you say, we have no mice; no cats. And that's how the unfortunate accident happened …

CAMILLA What accident?

PENELOPE Darlings, I'm forgetting your glasses.

CAMILLA What accident?

(Penelope turns to her; they look at each other for some time.)

Penelope …

PENELOPE *Life* – is by no means as straightforward as it's supposed to be.

RODGER If it wasn't a mouse, what were you aiming at?

PENELOPE You think we live in the age of reason, don't you? You think we can put our life under the microscope, prod it this way and that way with a little pair of tweezers and say: ah, yes; I did this because of this and this because of this. How simple!

RODGER Penelope, what ?

PENELOPE Ten years ago, on my way to visit a taxidermist, I got stuck in a lift between the fourth and fifth floors.

(Rodger scratches his head.)

Three-quarters of an hour later, coming down, between the fourth floor and the third floor, I got stuck in the same lift,

---

5 **by the same token** as a result of the same evidence – 17 **to prod** to push with a stick-like object – 18 **a pair of tweezers** a small tool for picking up or pulling out very small things, e.g. hairs from the eyebrows – 22 **taxidermist** ['tæksɪdɜːmɪst] a person who prepares and stuffs the skin of animals so that they look as if alive

together with the same stranger I was stuck in the lift with on the way up. Improbable? *Yes*. But it happened. That's what caused it ...

RODGER Caused what?

PENELOPE That's how I met Harry. And off went the chain of events on its immutable course. And what d'you think I had to do with it?

RODGER I don't get the drift ...

PENELOPE I mean we *pretend*, Rodger, we *pretend* ... that we're in control, that we decide ... Well maybe we do; but what makes us decide ...?

RODGER I don't agree with anything you're saying –

PENELOPE Of course you don't; you're not able to. You think we play our lives like fish.

RODGER Yes, like fish –

PENELOPE You think we stand on the banks of the river of life, all dressed up in our oilskins of habit, catching events like salmon as they leap past. It may seem so to you, Rodger; but are the events, in reality, catching us?

RODGER What *were* you aiming at?

(Pause)

PENELOPE Who, me ...?

(Slight pause)

RODGER Of course we're in control; we can choose, can't we?

PENELOPE D'you think I had a *choice* of marrying Harry or not marrying Harry?

---

6 **immutable** [ɪˈmjuːtəbl] unchangeable – 17 **oilskin** cloth treated with oil to make it waterproof

RODGER I'm not talking about Harry. I'm talking about life –

PENELOPE I'm talking about Harry. I had no choice.

RODGER Nonsense …

PENELOPE Of course I had no choice. We met, perforce, in a lift. And there we were later, drinking good coffee after a delicious meal in an expensive restaurant … It was a foregone conclusion; so much so that he didn't even bother to ask me; he *told* me. We'll get married, he said. Yes, I said, Naturally; of course; what else? Why not? … A dreadful gypsy violinist scraped his bow plaintively two tables away, while I sipped chartreuse; of course, why not, what else, who could think otherwise …?

RODGER You could have said no.

PENELOPE Of course I couldn't, how ridiculous.

RODGER I don't see anything ridiculous about it. Did he *force* you to say yes?

PENELOPE He didn't have to *force* me. I had no *choice*.

RODGER I don't understand.

PENELOPE I couldn't do otherwise.

RODGER I don't understand.

PENELOPE I *wanted* to.

RODGER You wanted to do otherwise?

PENELOPE *I wanted to marry Harry*.

RODGER Well there you are!

PENELOPE There you are.

---

4 **perforce** inevitably – 7 **a foregone conclusion** an inevitable result – 9 **gypsy** [ˈdʒɪpsɪ] a member of a wandering race, moving about in caravans and living in camps *(Zigeuner)* – 10 **scrape** to rub s.th. along some other instrument to produce a noise -plaintively sounding sad – 11 **chartreuse** [ʃɑːˈtrɜːz] *(alcoholic drink)*

RODGER And if you'd wanted to say no –

PENELOPE But I didn't want to say no … I wanted to say yes, I had no choice – but to want to say yes.

RODGER Then why blame Harry?

PENELOPE I'm not blaming Harry, why do you continually get the wrong end of the stick? I don't regret marrying him. Ours is not the kind of marriage one regrets. Far from it. Never once has Harry ever behaved in any way other than as I would have expected him to. Never once has he given me the slightest cause to feel he was dissatisfied or restless or wanted to see someone else's face at the breakfast table, just for once. Our life together has been one continuous stream of marital harmony …

CAMILLA Tell Rodger what you were aiming at, darling.

PENELOPE Aiming what at?

CAMILLA The revolver.

PENELOPE I wasn't aiming it. I just pointed it at something.

RODGER At what?

PENELOPE At a target.

RODGER Are you in the habit of doing target practice in the evening?

PENELOPE Habit has nothing to do with it. Besides, as I said, it was an accident.

CAMILLA Because you have no mice.

PENELOPE Yes, because I have no mice. And because plaster didn't fall from the ceiling and because the telephone didn't

---

6 **to get the wrong end of the stick** to misunderstand – 10 **dissatisfied** not content – 13 **marital** having to do with marriage – 19 **target** an aim in shooting practice, *also:* an object of attack – 25 **plaster** white material used to cover walls and ceilings

ring and because the world didn't suddenly come to an end; really, this is like an inquisition! One would think there were nothing else in the world but why I let off this silly gun! As though the whole Universe were centred in one accidental
revolver shot! Really, you're both positively *medieval*.

RODGER We don't have to stay if you don't want us to.

PENELOPE I do want you to. I want to be able to talk to friends intimate enough to understand without passing judgement.

RODGER What on?

PENELOPE Me.

CAMILLA Why should we?

PENELOPE Why indeed? Why should anyone pass judgement on anyone in this strange, haphazard, accidental life?

(Pause. A sob. Penelope is crying. Rodger flaps his arms.)

CAMILLA Penelope …

PENELOPE Don't speak to me. I don't want to be spoken to. I want absolute silence … I know I'm being incredibly tiresome.

RODGER Not at all –

PENELOPE Don't contradict me. I am … I'm being incredibly tiresome and gauche … Dragging you away from your television, as though real life is more important … I was brought up in the old-fashioned way, you see; to think of friends as friends. But of course it's all a mockery. Life isn't to be taken seriously. It's just a cheap imitation of a television play. So undramatic … The most incredible things happen

---

2 **inquisition** [ˌɪnkwɪˈzɪʃn] a thorough interrogation – 5 **positively** definitely – 5 **medieval** [ˌmedɪˈiːvl] belonging to the Middle Ages – 8 **intimate** [ˈɪntɪmɪt] very close (e.g. a friend) – 8 **to pass judgement on s.o.** to condemn s.o. – 13 **haphazard** [hæpˈhæzəd] happening by mere chance – 14 **to flap one's arms** to move one's arms up and down or from side to side – 21 **gauche** [gəʊʃ] tactless – 21 **to drag away** to pull away – 24 **mockery** a subject of laughter *(Hohn und Spott)*

suddenly out of the blue, as though they've been stuck in by accident, and the last act doesn't resolve a thing. Life is an affront to the intelligence, I realise that; badly written, badly acted, and apparently not directed at all …

5 RODGER I think you should take a sedative and go to bed.

PENELOPE What solution does that produce to which problem?

(Pause)

CAMILLA And you hit it.

10 PENELOPE Hit what?

CAMILLA The target.

PENELOPE What target?

CAMILLA The one you were aiming at.

PENELOPE I wasn't aiming at it, I just pointed the gun at it.

15 CAMILLA But you did.

PENELOPE Hit it?

CAMILLA Yes.

PENELOPE Yes.

CAMILLA Hm.

20 *(Pause)*

PENELOPE The first things I ever noticed about Harry were his intelligence and his poise. He was never surprised. This is a logical world, he used to say; why be surprised if one thing happens rather than another? If a lift breaks down there's
25 good reason for it. So while other men would have banged

---

1 **to stick in** to put in – 2 **to resolve** to bring about a result – 3 **affront** [əˈfrʌnt] deliberate show of disrespect, offence – 4 **to direct** to produce a play on the stage – 5 **sedative** [ˈsedətɪv] medicine which calms the nerves – 22 **poise** balance, self-confidence

on the sides with their fists and walked up and down and pressed all the buttons, Harry simply divided his *Times* in two, and he sat on the foreign news in one corner while I sat on the home news in another, and for the next twenty minutes he explained to me Einstein's Special Theory of Relativity. Life, Harry used to say, is reason. Quarrelling, Harry used to say, is the last resort of the feeble-minded. Surprise, hope and despair, Harry used to say, are the three ugly sisters in the tale of Man's quest towards intellectual maturity …

CAMILLA And down it fell …

PENELOPE Mine has been the perfect marriage!

RODGER Down what fell?

CAMILLA The target.

PENELOPE Yes, it fell down.

CAMILLA Lay down.

RODGER The target. Lay down?

PENELOPE Yes, Rodger, the target lay down.

RODGER I don't get the drift.

CAMILLA No, dear; you don't get the drift.

PENELOPE Because there isn't any drift to get.

(Pause)

CAMILLA You are so smug, Rodger.

RODGER What?

---

1 **to bang on s.th.** to beat s.th. with one's fists – 3 **foreign news/home news** *(two main parts of British daily newspapers)* – 7 **the feeble-minded** persons of inferior intelligence – 8 **despair** [dɪˈspeə] state of having lost all hope – 9 **quest** attempt to find s.th. – 10 **maturity** [məˈtjʊərɪtɪ] state of full development – 23 **smug** self-satisfied, too pleased with o.s.

CAMILLA You're so *smug*.

RODGER What are you talking about *now*?

CAMILLA You think nothing can ever happen to you. You think nothing can ever go wrong.

5 RODGER Of course it can't. I've explained. I'm impregnable.

CAMILLA You're insufferable.

RODGER I don't think you'd better have any more gin, dear …

CAMILLA Very well … I have a *lover*.

RODGER What the devil are you on about now?

10 CAMILLA I have a lover.

RODGER Nonsense; it's not your habit to –

CAMILLA Not my habit! You don't know anything about my habits! What do you think I think of when you're away, during the day? It's been my habit for years. What are you
15 smiling at? Haven't you noticed the gleam in my eye when you opened the door in the evening and said hallo, dear, and kissed me on the right cheek? Did you think my suppressed yawns were boredom? No, they were satiation.

RODGER I think you're going a bit far –

20 CAMILLA How often have I longed for a loaded revolver as you sat smugly asking if I'd had a good day?

RODGER *Really, Camilla* …

CAMILLA What do you know, Rodger? What do – you – know?

---

6 **insufferable** unbearable – 9 **what are you on about?** what are you talking about? – 15 **gleam** beam of soft ligh – 17 **suppressed yawns** attempts to prevent one's mouth from opening when tired or bored – 18 **satiation** [ˌseɪʃiˈeɪʃn] state of being oversatisfied

(Pause. Rodger picks up the revolver, goes over to Camilla, and puts it into her hand.)

RODGER Here you are. Hold it. Point it at me. I have the courage of my convictions. Pull back the safety catch. Pull the trigger.

(She pulls the trigger. Pause)

CAMILLA Oh dear …

(Pause)

I didn't have any lover … Is that how …?

PENELOPE Yes. That's how it happened to me.

4 **conviction** firm belief

Biographical Notes

James Saunders (1925 – 2004) was born in London. After finishing his studies at the University of Southampton he became a teacher of English. In 1949 he started writing plays, beginning with a few short pieces. But it was not until 1963 that he produced his first full- length play *Next Time I'll Sing to You* (the story of a hermit, who spent 36 years living in a hut in a field, cutting himself off from the outside world). This play investigates the essential loneliness of man and the general meaninglessness of his life. Similar problems are discussed in his 1964 collection *Neighbours & Other Plays*, which contains *A Slight Accident*. Most of these plays were written during the 1950s and are concerned with life's absurdity: *Alas, Poor Fred* examines the emptiness of marital life; *Neighbours* is a study of a confrontation between a black man and a white woman; *A Slight Accident* (first produced in 1961) is concerned with the conflict between the sense of planning one's own life and the inherent unpredictability of real-life events. It may also be seen as a study in the limitations and manipulation of language. His early plays made Saunders one of the main British exponents of the Theatre of the Absurd.

Saunders' reputation as one of Britains's top modern dramatists was further strengthened by *A Scent of Flowers* (1964/5), *The Borage Pigeon Affair* (1969), *Hans Kolhaas* (1972), *A Journey to London* (1975, co-author with John Vanbrugh), *Over the Wall* (1977) and *Random Moments in a May Garden* (1980).

He also wrote for television: *Watch me I'm a Bird* (1964) and the BBC series *Bloomers* (1979).

Harold Pinter
A Slight Ache

A country house, with two chairs and a table laid for breakfast at the centre of the stage. These will later be removed and the action will be focused on the scullery on the right and the study on the left, both indicated with a minimum of scenery and
5 *props. A large well kept garden is suggested at the back of the stage with flower beds, trimmed hedges, etc. The garden gate, which cannot be seen by the audience, is off right.*

Flora and Edward are discovered sitting at the breakfast table. Edward is reading the paper.

10 FLORA Have you noticed the honeysuckle this morning?

EDWARD The what?

FLORA The honeysuckle.

EDWARD Honeysuckle? Where?

FLORA By the back gate, Edward.

15 EDWARD Is that honeysuckle? I thought it was … convolvulus, or something.

FLORA But you know it's honeysuckle.

EDWARD I tell you I thought it was convolvulus.

(Pause)

20 FLORA It's in wonderful flower.

EDWARD I must look.

---

3 **focused** ['fəʊkəst] centred – 3 **scullery** a little room near the kitchen where dishes and pans are washed – 4 **study** a room used for studying and writing – 5 **props** (*short for:* stage properties) articles (e.g. pieces of furniture) used on stage – 10 **honeysuckle** (*Geißblatt*) – 15 **convolvulus** [kən'vɒlvjʊles] (*Winde*)

FLORA The whole garden's in flower this morning. The clematis. The convolvulus. Everything. I was out at seven. I stood by the pool.

EDWARD Did you say – that the convolvulus was in flower?

FLORA Yes.

EDWARD But good God, you just denied there was any.

FLORA I was talking about the honeysuckle.

EDWARD About the what?

FLORA *(calmly)* Edward – you know that shrub outside the toolshed …

EDWARD Yes, yes.

FLORA That's convolvulus.

EDWARD That?

FLORA Yes.

EDWARD Oh. *(Pause)* I thought it was japonica.

FLORA Oh, good Lord no.

EDWARD Pass the teapot, please.

(Pause. She pours tea for him.)

I don't see why I should be expected to distinguish between these plants. It's not my job.

FLORA You know perfectly well what grows in your garden.

EDWARD Quite the contrary. It is clear that I don't.

(Pause)

---

2 **clematis** [kliˈmeɪtɪs] (*Waldrebe*) – 9 **shrub** a low bush – 10 **toolshed** a small building in the garden where garden tools are kept – 15 **japonica** [dʒəˈpɒnɪkə] a type of ornamental bush

FLORA *(rising)* I was up at seven. I stood by the pool. The peace. And everything in flower. The sun was up. You should work in the garden this morning. We could put up the canopy.

EDWARD The canopy? What for?

FLORA To shade you from the sun.

EDWARD Is there a breeze?

FLORA A light one.

EDWARD It's very treacherous weather, you know.

(Pause)

FLORA Do you know what today is?

EDWARD Saturday.

FLORA It's the longest day of the year.

EDWARD Really?

FLORA It's the height of summer today.

EDWARD Cover the marmalade.

FLORA What?

EDWARD Cover the pot. There's a wasp. *(He puts the paper down on the table.)* Don't move. Keep still. What are you doing?

FLORA Covering the pot.

EDWARD Don't move. Leave it. Keep still.

(Pause)

---

4 **canopy** [ˈkænəpɪ] a hanging cover fixed above a seat – 7 **breeze** a light wind –
9 **treacherous** [ˈtretʃərəs] deceptive and dangerous – 15 **the height of summer** [haɪt] the longest day of summer – 18 **wasp** [wɒsp] a flying insect with a sting in the tail

Give me the "Telegraph".

FLORA Don't hit it. It'll bite.

EDWARD Bite? What do you mean, bite? Keep still. *(Pause)* It's landing.

FLORA It's going in the pot.

EDWARD Give me the lid.

FLORA It's in.

EDWARD Give me the lid.

FLORA I'll do it.

EDWARD Give it to me! Now … Slowly …

FLORA What are you doing?

EDWARD Be quiet. Slowly … carefully … on … the … pot! Ha-ha-ha. Very good.

(He sits on a chair to the right of the table.)

FLORA Now he's in the marmalade.

EDWARD Precisely.

(Pause. She sits on a chair to the left of the table and reads the "Telegraph".)

FLORA Can you hear him?

EDWARD Hear him?

FLORA Buzzing.

EDWARD Nonsense. How can you hear him? It's an earthenware lid.

FLORA He's becoming frantic.

---

1 **the 'Telegraph'** (*short for:* 'The Daily Telegraph') a British newspaper – 23 **earthenware** ['ɜːnweə] made of baked clay – 24 **frantic** wildly anxious

EDWARD Rubbish. Take it away from the table.

FLORA What shall I do with it?

EDWARD Put it in the sink and drown it.

FLORA It'll fly out and bite me.

5 EDWARD It will not bite you! Wasps don't bite. Anyway, it won't fly out. It's stuck. It'll drown where it is, in the marmalade.

FLORA What a horrible death.

EDWARD On the contrary.

(Pause)

10 FLORA Have you got something in your eyes?

EDWARD No. Why do you ask?

FLORA You keep clenching them, blinking them.

EDWARD I have a slight ache in them.

FLORA Oh dear.

15 EDWARD Yes, a slight ache. As if I hadn't slept.

FLORA Did you sleep, Edward?

EDWARD Of course I slept. Uninterrupted. As always.

FLORA And yet you feel tired.

EDWARD I didn't say I felt tired. I merely said I had a slight
20 ache in my eyes.

FLORA Why is that, then?

EDWARD I really don't know.

(Pause)

---

6 **stuck** unable to move – 12 **to clench** to close tightly – 12 **to blink one's eyes** to shut and open them quickly

FLORA Oh goodness!

EDWARD What is it?

FLORA I can see it. It's trying to come out.

EDWARD How can it?

FLORA Through the hole. It's trying to crawl out, through the spoon-hole.

EDWARD Mmmnn, yes. Can't do it, of course. *(Silent pause.)* Well, let's kill it, for goodness' sake.

FLORA Yes, let's. But how?

EDWARD Bring it out on the spoon and squash it on a plate.

FLORA It'll fly away. It'll bite.

EDWARD If you don't stop saying that word I shall leave this table.

FLORA But wasps do bite.

EDWARD They don't bite. They sting. It's snakes … that bite.

FLORA What about horseflies?

(Pause)

EDWARD *(to himself)* Horseflies suck.

(Pause)

FLORA *(tentatively)* If we … if we wait long enough, I suppose it'll choke to death. It'll suffocate in the marmalade.

EDWARD *(briskly)* You do know I've got work to do this morning, don't you? I can't spend the whole day worrying about a wasp.

---

10 **to squash** [ɒ] to press so as to kill – 18 **to suck** to draw liquid into the mouth – 20 **tentatively** hesitantly; here: in an uncertain voice – 21 **to choke** = **to suffocate** ['sʌfəkeɪt] to die because of lack of air – 22 **briskly** quickly

FLORA Well, kill it.

EDWARD You want to kill it?

FLORA Yes.

EDWARD Very well. Pass me the hot water jug.

5 FLORA What are you going to do?

EDWARD Scald it. Give it to me. *(She hands him the jug. Pause.)* Now …

FLORA *(whispering)* Do you want me to lift the lid?

EDWARD No, no, no. I'll pour down the spoon hole. Right …
10 down the spoon-hole.

FLORA Listen!

EDWARD What?

FLORA It's buzzing.

EDWARD Vicious creatures. *(Pause)* Curious, but I don't
15 remember seeing any wasps at all, all summer, until now. I'm sure I don't know why. I mean, there must have been wasps.

FLORA Please.

EDWARD This couldn't be the first wasp, could it?

20 FLORA Please.

EDWARD The first wasp of summer? No. It's not possible.

FLORA Edward.

EDWARD Mmmmnnn?

FLORA Kill it.

---

6 **to scald** [skɔːld] to hurt or kill by burning with hot liquid – 14 **vicious** [ˈvɪʃəs] cruel, dangerous

89

EDWARD   Ah, yes. Tilt the pot. Tilt. Aah … down here … right down … blinding him … that's … it.

FLORA   Is it?

EDWARD   Lift the lid. All right, I will. There he is! Dead. What a monster. *(He squashes it on a plate.)*

FLORA   What an awful experience.

EDWARD   What a beautiful day it is. Beautiful. I think I shall work in the garden this morning. Where's that canopy?

FLORA   It's in the shed.

EDWARD   Yes, we must get it out. My goodness, just look at that sky. Not a cloud. Did you say it was the longest day of the year today?

FLORA   Yes.

EDWARD   Ah, it's a good day. I feel it in my bones. In my muscles. I think I'll stretch my legs in a minute. Down to the pool. My God, look at that flowering shrub over there. Clematis. What a wonderful … *(He stops suddenly.)*

FLORA   What? *(Pause)* Edward, what is it? *(Pause)*

Edward …

EDWARD   *(thickly)* He's there.

FLORA   Who?

EDWARD   *(low, murmuring)* Blast and damn it, he's there, he's there at the back gate.

FLORA   Let me see. *(She moves over to him to look. Pause. Lightly)* Oh, it's the matchseller.

EDWARD   He's back again.

---

1 **to tilt s.th.** to cause s.th. to lean to one side – 22 **Blast and damn it** *(sl.) (a curse)*

FLORA But he's always there.

EDWARD Why? What is he doing there?

FLORA But he's never disturbed you, has he? The man's been standing there for weeks. You've never mentioned it.

EDWARD What is he doing there?

FLORA He's selling matches, of course.

EDWARD It's ridiculous. What's the time?

FLORA Half past nine.

EDWARD What in God's name is he doing with a tray full of matches at half past nine in the morning?

FLORA He arrives at seven o'clock.

EDWARD Seven o'clock?

FLORA He's always there at seven.

EDWARD Yes, but you've never … actually seen him arrive?

FLORA No, I …

EDWARD Well, how do you know he's … not been standing there all night?

(Pause)

FLORA Do you find him interesting, Edward?

EDWARD *(casually)* Interesting? No. No, I … don't find him interesting.

FLORA He's a very nice old man, really.

EDWARD You've spoken to him?

FLORA No. No, I haven't spoken to him. I've nodded.

EDWARD *(pacing up and down)* For two months he's been standing on that spot, do you realise that? Two months. I haven't been able to step outside the back gate.

FLORA Why on earth not?

EDWARD *(to himself)* It used to give me great pleasure, such pleasure, to stroll along through the long grass, out through the back gate, pass into the lane. That pleasure is now denied me. It's my own house, isn't it? It's my own gate.

FLORA I really can't understand this, Edward.

EDWARD Damn. And do you know I've never seen him sell one box? Not a box. It's hardly surprising. He's on the wrong road. It's not a road at all. What is it? It's a lane, leading to the monastery. Off everybody's route. Even the monks take a short cut to the village, when they want to go … to the village. No one goes up it. Why doesn't he stand on the main road if he wants to sell matches, by the *front* gate? The whole thing's preposterous.

FLORA *(going over him)* I don't know why you're getting so excited about it. He's a quiet, harmless old man, going about his business. He's quite harmless.

EDWARD I didn't say he wasn't harmless. Of course he's harmless. How could he be other than harmless?

(Fade out and silence)

(Flora's voice, far in the house, drawing nearer)

FLORA *(off)* Edward, where are you? Edward? Where are you, Edward? *(She appears.)* Edward? Edward, what are you doing in the scullery?

---

6 **to stroll along** [strəʊl] to walk without haste – 7 **lane** a narrow road between fields, walls, hedges, etc. – 13 **monastery** ['mɒnəstrɪ] a building in which monks live – 14 **short cut** ['-,-] a route that is quicker than the usual one – 17 **preposterous** [prɪ'pɒstərəs] absurd, completely unreasonable – 22 **other than** anything but

EDWARD *(looking through the scullery window)* Doing?

FLORA I've been looking everywhere for you. I put up the canopy ages ago. I came back and you were nowhere to be seen. Have you been out?

5 EDWARD No.

FLORA Where have you been?

EDWARD Here.

FLORA I looked in your study. I even went into the attic.

EDWARD *(tonelessly)* What would I be doing in the attic?

10 FLORA I couldn't imagine what had happened to you. Do you know it's twelve o'clock?

EDWARD Is it?

FLORA I even went to the bottom of the garden, to see if you were in the toolshed.

15 EDWARD *(tonelessly)* What would I be doing in the toolshed?

FLORA You must have seen me in the garden. You can see through this window.

EDWARD Only part of the garden.

FLORA Yes.

20 EDWARD Only a corner of the garden. A very small corner.

FLORA What are you doing here?

EDWARD Nothing. I was digging out some notes, that's all.

FLORA Notes?

EDWARD For my essay.

---

8 **attic** a room immediately below the roof – 22 **to dig out** to find by searching

FLORA Which essay?

EDWARD My essay on space and time.

FLORA But … I've never … I don't know that one.

EDWARD You don't know it?

FLORA I thought you were writing one about the Belgian Congo.

EDWARD I've been engaged on the dimensionality and continuity of space … and time … for years.

FLORA And the Belgian Congo?

EDWARD *(shortly)* Never mind about the Belgian Congo.

(Pause)

FLORA But you don't keep notes in the scullery.

EDWARD You'd be surprised. You'd be highly surprised.

FLORA Good Lord, what's that? Is that a bullock let loose? No. It's the matchseller! My goodness, you can see him … through the hedge. He looks bigger. Have you been watching him? He looks … like a bullock. *(Pause)* Edward? *(Pause. Moving over to him)* Are you coming outside? I've put up the canopy. You'll miss the best of the day. You can have an hour before lunch.

EDWARD I've no work to do this morning.

FLORA What about your essay? You don't intend to stay in the scullery all day, do you?

EDWARD Get out. Leave me alone.

(A slight pause)

6 **Belgian Congo** *now:* Democratic Republic of the Congo – 7 **dimensionality** [dɪmenʃə'næləti] – 8 **continuity** [ˌkɒntɪ'njuːəti] the state of being continuous, uninterrupted – 14 **bullock** ['bʊlək] a young bull

FLORA Really Edward. You've never spoken to me like that in all your life.

EDWARD Yes, I have.

FLORA Oh, Weddie. Beddie-Weddie..

EDWARD Do not call me that!

FLORA Your eyes are bloodshot.

EDWARD Damn it.

FLORA It's too dark in here to peer …

EDWARD Damn.

FLORA It's so bright outside.

EDWARD Damn.

FLORA And it's dark in here.

(Pause)

EDWARD Christ blast it!

FLORA You're frightened of him.

EDWARD I'm not.

FLORA You're frightened of a poor old man. Why?

EDWARD I am not!

FLORA He's a poor, harmless old man.

EDWARD Aaah my eyes.

FLORA Let me bathe them.

EDWARD Keep away. *(Pause. Slowly)* I want to speak to that man. I want to have a word with him. *(Pause)*

---

6 **bloodshot** *of eyes:* red – 8 **to peer** to look very carefully – 14 **Christ blast it!** *(a curse)*

It's quite absurd, of course. I really can't tolerate something so absurd, right on my doorstep. I shall not tolerate it. He's sold nothing all morning. No one passed. Yes. A monk passed. A non-smoker. In a loose garment. It's quite obvious he was a non-smoker but still, the man made no effort.

He made no effort to clinch a sale, to rid himself of one of his cursed boxes. His one chance, all morning, and he made no effort.

(Pause)

I haven't wasted my time. I've hit, in fact, upon the truth. He's not a matchseller at all. The bastard isn't a matchseller at all. Curious I never realised that before. He's an impostor. I watched him very closely. He made no move towards the monk. As for the monk, the monk made no move towards him. The monk was moving along the lane. He didn't pause, or halt, or in any way alter his step. As for the matchseller – how ridiculous to go on calling him by that title. What a farce. No, there is something very false about that man. I intend to get to the bottom of it. I'll soon get rid of him. He can go and ply his trade somewhere else. Instead of standing like a bullock … a bullock, outside my back gate.

FLORA But if he isn't a matchseller, what is his trade?

EDWARD We'll soon find out.

FLORA You're going out to speak to him?

EDWARD Certainly not! Go out to *him*? Certainly … not. I'll invite him in here. Into my study. Then we'll … get to the bottom of it.

FLORA Why don't you call the police and have him removed?

---

4 **garment** an article of clothing – 6 **to clinch a sale** *(coll.)* to sell something – 6 **to rid o.s. of s.th.** to get rid of s.th.; *here:* to sell – 7 **cursed** [kɜːst] damned – 12 **impostor** [ɪmˈpɒstə] a person who deceives others by pretending to be s.o. or s.th. else – 16 **to alter** [ˈɔːltə] to change – 19 **to get to the bottom of s.th.** to inquire into the cause of s.th. – 20 **to ply one's trade** to go about one's business

(He laughs. Pause)

Why don't you call the police, Edward? You could say he was a public nuisance. Although I … I can't say I find him a nuisance.

EDWARD Call him in.

FLORA Me?

EDWARD Go out and call him in.

FLORA Are you serious? *(Pause)* Edward, I could call the police. Or even the vicar.

EDWARD Go and get him.

(She goes out. Silence. Edward waits.)

FLORA *(in the garden)* Good morning.

(Pause)

We haven't met. I live in this house here. My husband and I.

(Pause)

I wonder if you could … would you care for a cup of tea?

(Pause)

Or a glass of lemon? It must be so dry, standing here.

(Pause)

Would you like to come inside for a little while? It's much cooler. There's something we'd very much like to … tell you, that will benefit you. Could you spare a few moments? We won't keep you long.

(Pause)

---

3 **public nuisance** ['njuːsns] person who behaves in such a way as to be troublesome to others − 9 **vicar** ['vɪkə] a priest in charge of a church − 22 **to benefit s.o.** to be useful to s.o.

Might I buy your tray of matches, do you think? We've run out, completely, and we always keep a very large stock. It happens that way, doesn't it? Well, we can discuss it inside. Do come. This way. Ah now, do come. Our house is full of curios, you know. My husband's been rather a collector. We have goose for lunch. Do you care for goose? *(She moves to the gate.)* Come and have lunch with us. This way. That's … right. May I take your arm? There's a good deal of *nettle* inside the gate. *(The matchseller appears.)* Here. This way. Mind now. Isn't it beautiful weather? It's the longest day of the year today.

(Pause)

That's honeysuckle. And that's convolvulus. There's clematis. And do you see that plant by the conservatory? That's japonica.

(Silence. She enters the study.)

FLORA   He's here.

EDWARD   I know.

FLORA   He's in the hall.

EDWARD   I know he's here. I can smell him.

FLORA   Smell him?

EDWARD   I smelt him when he came under my window. Can't you smell the house now?

FLORA   What are you going to do with him, Edward? You won't be rough with him in any way? He's very old. I'm not sure if he can hear, or even see. And he's wearing the oldest -

EDWARD   I don't want to know what he's wearing.

2 **to run out of s.th.** to have no more of s.th. – 2 **stock** supply – 5 **curio** (*short for:* curiosity) an object that is interesting because it is rare or unusual – 8 **nettle** wild plant *(Brennessel)* – 10 **to mind** *here:* to pay attention, to be careful – 14 **conservatory** [kənˈsɜːvətrɪ] glass house

FLORA But you'll see for yourself in a minute, if you speak to him.

EDWARD I shall.

(Slight pause)

5 FLORA He's an old man. You won't … be rough with him?

EDWARD If he's so old, why doesn't he seek shelter … from the storm?

FLORA But there's no storm. It's summer, the longest day …

EDWARD There was a storm, last week. A summer storm. He
10 stood without moving, while it raged about him.

FLORA When was this?

EDWARD He remained quite still, while it thundered all about him.

(Pause)

15 FLORA Edward … are you sure it's wise to bother about all this?

EDWARD Tell him to come in.

FLORA I…

EDWARD Now.

20 *(She goes and collects the matchseller.)*

FLORA Hullo. Would you like to go in? I won't be long. Up these stairs here. *(Pause)* You can have some sherry before lunch. *(Pause)* Shall I take your tray? No. Very well, take it with you. Just … up those stairs. The door at the … *(She
25 watches him move.)* the door … *(Pause)* the door at the top. I'll join you … later.

6 **shelter** protection – 10 **to rage** *of storms:* to be very violent

(She goes out.)

(The matchseller stands on the threshold of the study.)

EDWARD *(cheerfully)* Here I am. Where are you?

(Pause)

Don't stand out there, old chap. Come into my study. *(He rises.)* Come in.

(The matchseller enters.)

That's right. Mind how you go. That's … it. Now, make yourself comfortable. Thought you might like some refreshment, on a day like this. Sit down, old man. What will you have? Sherry? Or what about a double scotch? Eh?

(Pause)

I entertain the villagers annually, as a matter of fact. I'm not the squire, but they look upon me with some regard. Don't believe we've got a squire here any more, actually. Don't know what became of him. Nice old man he was.

Great chess-player, as I remember. Three daughters. The pride of the county. Flaming red hair. Alice was the eldest. Sit yourself down, old chap. Eunice I think was number two. The youngest one was the best of the bunch. Sally. No, no, wait a minute, no, it wasn't Sally, it was … Fanny. Fanny. A flower. You must be a stranger here. Unless you lived here once, went on a long voyage and have lately returned. Do you know the district?

(Pause)

Now, now, you mustn't … stand about like that. Take a seat. Which one would you prefer? We have a great variety, as you

---

2 **threshold** [ˈθreʃhəʊld] plank under a doorway, entrance – 5 **chap** *(coll.)* fellow, old friend – 13 **to entertain** *here:* to provide food and drink at a party – 14 **squire** the main landowner in a village – 14 **regard** *here:* respect – 19 **Eunice** [ˈjuːnɪs] – 20 **bunch** *(coll.)* group

see. Can't stand uniformity. Like different seats, different backs. Often when I'm working, you know, I draw up one chair, scribble a few lines, put it by, draw up another, sit back, ponder, put it by … *(absently)* … sit back … put it by…

(Pause)

I write theological and philosophical essays …

(Pause)

Now and again I jot down a few observations on certain tropical phenomena – not from the same standpoint, of course. *(Silent pause)* Yes. Africa, now. Africa's always been my happy hunting ground. Fascinating country. Do you know it? I get the impression that you've … been around a bit. Do you by any chance know the Membunza Mountains? Great range south of Katambaloo. French Equatorial Africa, if my memory serves me right. Most extraordinary diversity of flora and fauna. Especially fauna. I understand in the Gobi Desert you can come across some very strange sights. Never been there myself. Studied the maps though. Fascinating things, maps.

(Pause)

Do you live in the village? I don't often go down, of course. Or are you passing through? On your way to another part of the country? Well, I can tell you, in my opinion you won't find many prettier parts than here. We win the first prize regularly, you know, the best kept village in the area. Sit down.

(Pause)

I say, can you hear me?

(Pause)

---

3 **to scribble** to write very quickly – 3 **to put s.th. by** to put s.th. aside – 8 **to jot s.th. down** to write s.th. down hurriedly – 9 **phenomena** *(pl.)* [fəˈnɒmɪnə] *(sg.* phenomenon) – 16 **to understand** *here:* to have been informed

I said, I say, can you hear me?

(Pause)

You possess most extraordinary repose, for a man of your age, don't you? Well, perhaps that's not quite the right word … repose. Do you find it chilly in here? I'm sure it's chillier in here than out. I haven't been out yet, today, though I shall probably spend the whole afternoon working, in the garden, under my canopy, at my table, by the pool.

(Pause)

Oh, I understand you met my *wife*? Charming woman, don't you think? Plenty of grit there, too. Stood by me through thick and thin, that woman. In season and out of season. Fine figure of a woman she was, too, in her youth. Wonderful carriage, flaming red hair. *(He stops abruptly.)*

(Pause)

Yes, I … I was in much the same position myself then as you are now, you understand. Struggling to make my way in the world. I was in commerce too. *(With a chuckle)* Oh, yes, I know what it's like – the weather, the rain, beaten from pillar to post, up hill and down dale … the rewards were few … winters in hovels … up till all hours working at your thesis … yes, I've done it all. Let me advise you. Get a good woman to stick by you. Never mind what the world says. Keep at it. Keep your shoulder to the wheel. It'll pay dividends.

(Pause)

---

3 **repose** [rɪˈpəʊz] quiet manner that doesn't betray any feelings – 5 **chilly** cold – 11 **grit** great courage; determination – 12 **in season and out of season** at any time – 14 **carriage** [ˈkærɪdʒ] *here:* the way a person stands and walks – 18 **chuckle** a quiet laugh – 20 **from pillar to post** from one place to another – 20 **up hill and down dale** *(poet.)* up the hills and down to the valley – 21 **hovel** [ˈhɒvl] miserable place to live in – 21 **thesis** a long article written for a university degree – 25 **to keep one's shoulder to the wheel** to make an effort, to go on working – 25 **to pay dividends** to produce a benefit, an advantage

(With a laugh.) You must excuse my chatting away like this. We have few visitors this time of the year. All our friends summer abroad. I'm a home bird myself. Wouldn't mind taking a trip to Asia Minor, mind you, or to certain lower regions of the Congo, but Europe? Out of the question. Much too noisy. I'm sure you agree. Now look, what will you have to drink? A glass of ale? Curaçao Fockink Orange? Ginger beer? Tia Maria? A Wachenheimer Fuchsmantel Riesling Beerenauslese? Gin and it? Chateauneuf-du-Pape? A little Asti Spumante? Or what do you say to a straightforward Piesporter Goldtröpfchen Feine Auslese (Reichsgraf von Kesselstaff)? Any preference?

(Pause)

You look a trifle warm. Why don't you take off your balaclava? I'd find that a little itchy myself. But then I've always been one for freedom of movement. Even in the depth of winter I wear next to nothing.

(Pause)

I say, can I ask you a personal question? I don't want to seem inquisitive but aren't you rather on the wrong road for matchselling? Not terribly busy, is it? Of course you may not care for petrol fumes or the noise of traffic. I can quite understand that.

(Pause)

Do forgive me peering but is that a glass eye you're wearing?

(Pause)

---

1 **to chat away** to talk continuously without a clear purpose – 3 **to summer** *(rare)* to spend the summer – 4 **Asia Minor** [ˈeɪʒəˈmaɪnə] *(Kleinasien)* – 4 **mind you** believe me – 9 **gin and it** gin and vermouth – 14 **a trifle warm** rather warm – 15 **balaclava** [ˌbæləˈklɑːvə] a warm woollen headcovering that leaves the face free, but covers the head, ears, and neck – 15 **itchy** tickling in an annoying way – 17 **next to nothing** almost nothing – 20 **inquisitive** [ɪnˈkwɪzətɪv] eager to learn details about other people's affairs – 22 **petrol fumes** nasty-smelling gases coming from cars

Do take off your balaclava, there's a good chap, put your tray down and take your ease, as they say in this part of the world. *(He moves towards him.)* I must say you keep quite a good stock, don't you? Tell me, between ourselves, are those boxes full, or are there just a few half-empty ones among them? Oh yes, I used to be in commerce. Well now, before the good lady sounds the gong for petit déjeuner will you join me in an apéritif? I recommend a glass of cider. Now … just a minute … I know I've got some – Look out! Mind your tray!

(The tray falls, and the matchboxes.)

Good God, what …?

(Pause)

You've dropped your tray.

(Pause. He picks the matchboxes up.)

(Grunts) Eh, these boxes are all wet. You've no right to sell wet matches, you know. Uuuuugggh. This feels suspiciously like fungus. You won't get very far in this trade if you don't take care of your goods. *(Grunts, rising.)* Well, here you are.

(Pause)

Here's your tray.

(He puts the tray into the matchseller's hands, and sits. Pause)

Now listen, let me be quite frank with you, shall I? I really cannot understand why you don't sit down. There are four chairs at your disposal. Not to mention the hassock. I can't possibly talk to you unless you're settled. Then and only then can I speak to you. Do you follow me? You're not being

---

2 **there's a good chap** *(a phrase expressing satisfaction with someone's behaviour, esp. that of obedient children or dogs)* – 19 **fungus** [ˈfʌŋɡəs] a soft whitish growth that forms on old food, etc. – 24 **frank** sincere, open – 26 **hassock** a small bench for kneeling on *(in church, etc.)*

terribly helpful. *(Slight pause.)* You're sweating. The sweat's pouring out of you. Take off that balaclava.

(Pause)

Go into the corner then. Into the corner. Go on. Get into the shade of the corner. Back. Backward.

(Pause)

Get back!

(Pause)

Ah, you understand me. Forgive me for saying so, but I had decided that you had the comprehension of a bullock. I was mistaken. You understand me perfectly well. That's right. A little more. A little to the right. Aaah. Now you're there. In shade, in shadow. Good-o. Now I can get down to brass tacks. Can't I?

(Pause)

No doubt you're wondering why I invited you into this house? You may think I was alarmed by the look of you. You would be quite mistaken. I was not alarmed by the look of you. I did not find you at all alarming. No, no.
Nothing outside this room has ever alarmed me. You disgusted me, quite forcibly, if you want to know the truth.

(Pause)

Why did you disgust me to that extent? That seems to be a pertinent question. You're no more disgusting than Fanny, the squire's daughter, after all. In appearance you differ but not in essence. There's the same …

---

14 **to get down to brass tacks** *(coll.)* to start talking about the really important problems – 22 **to disgust s.o.** to cause a feeling of strong dislike in s.o. – 22 **forcibly** strongly – 25 **pertinent** relevant – 27 **in essence** ['esns] in one's inner nature – 5 **from dawn till dusk** from daybreak to nightfall

(Pause)

The same …

(Pause)

(In a low voice) I want to ask you a question. Why do you stand outside my back gate, from dawn till dusk, why do you pretend to sell matches, why …? What is it, damn you. You're shivering. You're sagging. Come here, come here … mind your tray! *(Edward rises and moves behind a chair.)* Come, quick quick. There. Sit here. Sit … sit in this.

(The matchseller stumbles and sits. Pause)

Aaaah! You're sat. At last. What a relief. You must be tired. *(Slight pause)* Chair comfortable? I bought it in a sale. I bought all the furniture in this house in a sale. The same sale. When I was a young man. You too, perhaps. You too, perhaps.

(Pause)

At the same time, perhaps!

(Pause)

(Muttering) I must get some air. I must get a breath of air. *(He goes to the door.)* Flora!

FLORA Yes?

EDWARD *(with great weariness)* Take me into the garden.

(Silence. They move from the study door to a chair under a canopy.)

FLORA Come under the canopy.

---

6 **damn you** *(sl.) (a strong way of expressing surprise, anger, etc.)* – 7 **to shiver** to tremble from cold or fear – 7 **to sag** to sink down slowly – 11 **you're sat** you are seated – 12 **sale** *here:* auction – 22 **with great weariness** ['wɪərɪnɪs] expressing extreme tiredness

EDWARD Ah. *(He sits.)*

(Pause)

The peace. The peace out here.

FLORA Look at our trees.

5 EDWARD Yes.

FLORA Our own trees. Can you hear the birds?

EDWARD No, I can't hear them.

FLORA But they're singing, high up, and flapping.

EDWARD Good. Let them flap.

10 FLORA Shall I bring your lunch out here? You can have it in peace, and a quiet drink, under your canopy.

(Pause)

How are you getting on with your old man?

EDWARD What do you mean?

15 FLORA What's happening? How are you getting on with him?

EDWARD Very well. We get on remarkably well. He's a little … reticent. Somewhat withdrawn. It's understandable. I should be the same, perhaps, in his place. Though, of course, I could not possibly find myself in his place.

20 FLORA Have you found out anything about him?

EDWARD A little. A little. He's had various trades, that's certain. His place of residence is unsure. He's … he's not a drinking man. As yet, I haven't discovered the reason for his arrival here. I shall in due course … by nightfall.

25 FLORA Is it necessary?

---

8 **to flap** to move (the wings) up and down – 17 **reticent** ['retɪsənt] shy and silent – 17 **withdrawn** habitually quiet, not concerned with what other people say – 24 **in due course** at the appropriate time

EDWARD Necessary?

FLORA *(quickly sitting on the right arm of the chair)* I could show him out now, it wouldn't matter. You've seen him, he's harmless, unfortunate … old, that's all. Edward – listen – he's not here through any … design, or anything, I know it. I mean, he might just as well stand outside our back gate as anywhere else. He'll move on. I can … make him. I promise you. There's no point in upsetting yourself like this. He's an old man, weak in the head … that's all.

(Pause)

EDWARD You're deluded.

FLORA Edward –

EDWARD *(rising)* You're deluded. and stop calling me Edward.

FLORA You're not still frightened of him?

EDWARD Frightened of him? Of *him*? Have you *seen* him?

(Pause)

He's like jelly. A great bullockfat of jelly. He can't see straight. I think as a matter of fact he wears a glass eye. He's almost stone deaf … almost … not quite. He's very nearly dead on his feet. Why should he frighten me? No, you're a woman, you know nothing. *(Slight pause.)* But he possesses other faculties. Cunning. The man's an impostor and he knows I know it.

FLORA I'll tell you what. Look. Let me speak to him. I'll speak to him.

EDWARD *(quietly)* And I know he knows I know it.

---

3 **to show s.o. out** to accompany s.o. to the door – 5 **design** *here:* evil purpose, intention, plan – 11 **deluded** misled, mistaken – 17 **jelly** a sweet soft food substance that shakes when moved; *here:* any semi-solid substance – 17 **bullockfat** a heap of fat as big as a bullock – 20 **to be dead on one's feet** to be too exhausted to stand on one's feet – 22 **cunning** cleverness in deceiving

FLORA I'll find out all about him, Edward. I promise you I will.

EDWARD And he knows I know.

FLORA Edward! Listen to me! I can find out all about him, I promise you. I shall go and have a word with him now. I shall … get to the bottom of it.

EDWARD You? It's laughable.

FLORA You'll see – he won't bargain for me. I'll surprise him. He'll … he'll admit everything.

EDWARD *(softly)* He'll admit everything, will he?

FLORA You wait and see, you just –

EDWARD *(hissing)* What are you plotting?

FLORA I know exactly what I shall –

EDWARD What are you plotting? *(He seizes her arms.)*

FLORA Edward, you're hurting me!

(Pause)

(With dignity) I shall wave from the window when I'm ready. Then you can come up. I shall get to the truth of it, I assure you. You're much too heavy-handed, in every way. You should trust your wife more, Edward. You should trust her judgement, and have a greater insight into her capabilities. A woman … a woman will often succeed, you know, where a man must invariably fail.

(Silence. She goes into the study.)

Do you mind if I come in?

(The door closes.)

---

7 **to bargain for s.o. or s.th.** to be prepared for s.o. or s.th. – 11 **to plot** to plan secretly – 18 **heavy-handed** not skilful, not careful

Are. you comfortable? *(Pause)* Oh, the sun's shining directly on you. Wouldn't you rather sit in the shade? *(She sits down.)*

It's the longest day of the year today, did you know that? Actually the year has flown. I can remember Christmas and that dreadful frost. And the floods! I hope you weren't here in the floods. We were out of danger up here, of course, but in the valleys whole families I remember drifted away on the current. The country was a lake. Everything stopped. We lived on our own preserves, drank elderberry wine, studied other cultures.

(Pause)

Do you know, I've got a feeling I've seen you before, somewhere. Long before the flood. You were much younger. Yes, I'm really sure of it. Between ourselves, were you ever a poacher? I had an encounter with a poacher once. It was a ghastly rape, the brute. High up on a hillside cattle track. Early spring. I was out riding on my pony. And there on the verge a man lay – ostensibly injured, lying on his front, I remember, possibly the victim of a murderous assault, how was I to know? I dismounted, I went to him, he rose, I fell, my pony took off, down to the valley. I saw the sky through the trees, blue. Up to my ears in mud. It was a desperate battle.

(Pause)

I lost.

(Pause)

---

4 **actually** really – 4 **to fly** *here:* to pass very quickly – 8 **current** [ˈkʌrənt] a continuously moving mass of water – 9 **preserves** food that can be kept for a long time by a special treatment *(Eingemachtes)* – 9 **elderberry** *(Holunderbeere)* – 15 **poacher** person who hunts illegally – 15 **encounter** a sudden or unexpected meeting – 16 **ghastly** terrible – 16 **rape** crime of having sex with a woman against her will – 16 **brute** a brutal person – 18 **verge** the border of a road or path – 18 **ostensibly** apparently but not really – 19 **assault** attack – 20 **to dismount** to get down from one's horse

Of course, life was perilous in those days. It was my first canter unchaperoned.

(Pause)

Years later, when I was a Justice of the Peace for the county, I had him in front of the bench. He was there for poaching. That's how I know he was a poacher. The evidence though was sparse, inadmissible, I acquitted him, letting him off with a caution. He'd grown a red beard, I remember. Yes. A bit of a stinker.

(Pause)

I say, you are perspiring, aren't you? Shall I mop your brow? With my chiffon? Is it the heat? Or the closeness? Or confined space? Or …? *(She goes over to him.)* Actually, the day is cooling. It'll soon be dusk. Perhaps it is dusk. May I? You don't mind?

(Pause. She mops his brow.)

Ah, there, that's better. And your cheeks. It is a woman's job, isn't it? And I'm the only woman on hand. There.

(Pause. She leans on the arm of chair.)

(Intimately) Tell me, have you a woman? Do you like women? Do you ever … think about women?

(Pause) Have you ever … stopped a woman? *(Pause)*

---

1 **perilous** dangerous – 2 **my first canter unchaperoned** [ʌnˈʃæpərəʊnd] my first ride without an older person to accompany and protect me – 4 **Justice of the Peace** person acting as a judge in the lowest courts – 5 **bench** *here:* the seat of a judge – 7 **sparse** *here:* scanty, not sufficient – 7 **inadmissible** that cannot be allowed – 7 **to acquit** to declare a person not guilty – 8 **caution** *here:* a warning given by a judge – 9 **stinker** *(sl.)* a mean or despicable person – 11 **to perspire** to sweat – 11 **to mop** to dry by rubbing with cloth – 12 **chiffon** [ˈʃɪfɒn] scarf made of thin material – 12 **closeness** condition of being warm and humid – 13 **confined** limited

I'm sure you must have been quite attractive once. *(She sits.)* Not any more, of course. You've got a vile smell. Vile. Quite repellent, in fact.

(Pause)

5 Sex, I suppose, means nothing to you. Does it ever occur to you that sex is a very vital experience for other people? Really, I think you'd amuse me if you weren't so hideous. You're probably quite amusing in your own way. *(Seductively)* Tell me all about love. Speak to me of love.

10 *(Pause)*

God knows what you're saying at this very moment. It's quite disgusting. Do you know when I was a girl I loved … I loved … I simply adored … what *have* you got on, for goodness sake? A jersey? It's clogged. Have you been rolling in mud?
15 *(Slight pause)* You haven't been rolling in mud, have you? *(She rises and goes over to him.)* And what have you got under your jersey? Let's see. *(Slight pause)* I'm not tickling you, am I? No. Good … Lord, is this a vest? That's quite original. Quite original. *(She sits on the arm of his chair.)*
20 Hmmnn, you're a solid old boy, I must say. Not at all like a jelly. All you need is a bath. A lovely lathery bath. And a good scrub. A lovely lathery scrub. *(Pause)* Don't you? It will be a pleasure. *(She throws her arms round him.)* I'm going to keep you. I'm going to keep you, you dreadful chap, and call you
25 Barnabas. Isn't it dark, Barnabas? Your eyes, your eyes, your great big eyes.

(Pause)

My husband would never have guessed your name. Never. *(She kneels at his feet. Whispering)* It's me you were waiting

---

2 **vile** unpleasant, nasty – 3 **repellent** causing dislike – 6 **vital** important – 7 **hideous** [ˈhɪdɪəs] extremely ugly, repellent – 9 **seductively** *here:* in a voice that contains an invitation to sex – 14 **jersey** a warm woollen pullover – 14 **clogged** covered with dirt – 18 **vest** a sleeveless undergarment – 21 **lathery** [ˈlɑːðərɪ] full of foam produced by the mixture of soap and water – 22 **scrub** the act of cleaning by hard rubbing

for, wasn't it? You've been standing waiting for me. You've seen me in the woods, picking daisies, in my apron, my pretty daisy apron, and you came and stood, poor creature, at my gate, till death us do part. Poor Barnabas. I'm going to put you to bed. I'm going to put you to bed and watch over you. But first you must have a good whacking great bath. And I'll buy you pretty little things that will suit you. And little toys to play with. On your deathbed. Why shouldn't you die happy?

(A shout from the hall)

EDWARD Well? *(Footsteps upstage.)* Well?

FLORA Don't come in.

EDWARD Well?

FLORA He's dying.

EDWARD Dying? He's not dying.

FLORA I tell you, he's very ill.

EDWARD He's not dying! Nowhere near. He'll see you cremated.

FLORA The man is desperately ill!

EDWARD Ill? You lying slut. Get back to your trough!

FLORA Edward …

EDWARD *(violently)* To your trough!

(She goes out. Pause)

---

2 **daisy** a small white flower *(Gänseblümchen)* – 4 **till death us do part** till death separates us (part of the pledge taken by bride and bridegroom during the marriage ceremony in church) – 6 **whacking** *(coll.)* very big – 17 **nowhere near** *here:* not at all – 18 **to cremate s.o.** [krɪˈmeɪt] to burn s.o. at a special funeral ceremony – **He'll see you cremated.** He'll outlive you. – 20 **slut** a woman who acts immorally – 20 **trough** [trɒf] a long narrow object for holding food or water for animals

(Coolly) Good evening to you. Why are you sitting in the gloom? Oh, you've begun to disrobe. Too warm? Let's open these windows, then, what? *(He opens the windows.)* Pull the blinds. *(He pulls the blinds.)* And close … the curtains … again. *(He closes the curtains.)* Ah. Air will enter through the side chinks. Of the blinds. And filter through the curtains. I hope. Don't want to suffocate, do we?

(Pause)

More comfortable? Yes. You look different in darkness. Take off all your togs, if you like. Make yourself at home. Strip to your buff. Do as you would in your own house.

(Pause)

Did you say something?

(Pause)

Did you say something?

(Pause)

Anything? Well then, tell me about your boyhood. Mmnn?

(Pause)

What did you do with it? Run? Swim? Kick the ball? You kicked the ball? What position? Left back? Goalie? First reserve?

(Pause)

I used to play myself. Country house matches, mostly. Kept wicket and batted number seven.

(Pause)

2 **gloom** semi-darkness – 2 **to disrobe** to undress – 4 **blinds** cloth or other material pulled down from a roller to cover a window – 6 **chink** narrow opening in the blinds – 10 **togs** *(coll.)* clothes – 11 **to strip to the buff** *(coll.)* to take off all clothes – 20 **goalie** *(coll.)* goalkeeper – 24 **wicket** *in cricket:* three upright sticks which the batsman tries to defend and the bowler tries to hit – **to keep wicket** to act as the player who stands behind the wicket to catch the ball

Kept wicket and batted number seven. Man called – Cavendish, I think had something of your style. Bowled left arm over the wicket, always kept his cap on, quite a dab hand at solo whist, preferred a good round of prop and cop to anything else.

(Pause)

On wet days when the field was swamped.

(Pause)

Perhaps you don't play cricket.

(Pause)

Perhaps you never met Cavendish and never played cricket. You look less and less like a cricketer the more I see of you. Where did you live in those days? God damn it, I'm entitled to know something about you! You're in my blasted house, on my territory, drinking my wine, eating my duck! Now you've had your filll you sit like a hump, a mouldering heap. In my room. My den. I can rem … *(He stops abruptly.)*

(Pause)

You find that funny? Are you grinning?

(Pause)

(In disgust) Good Christ, is that a grin on your face? *(Further disgust)* It's lopsided. It's all – down on one side. You're grinning. It amuses you, does it? When I tell you how well I remember this room, how well I remember this den.

---

1 **to bat** *in cricket:* to hit the ball – 3 **bowled left arm** threw the ball over his shoulder with a straight left arm – 4 **to be a dab hand at** *(coll.)* to be very clever or good at – 4 **solo whist** a card game – 4 **prop and cop** a special way to play solo whist – 7 **swamped** [ɒ] too wet to play on – 13 **to be entitled** to to have the right to – 14 **blasted** damned – 16 **to have one's fill** to eat and drink as much as one can – 16 **hump** shapeless mass – 16 **to moulder** to decay slowly (like a corpse) – 17 **den** a room in which one works, study – 22 **lopsided** having one side heavier or lower than the other

(Muttering) Ha. Yesterday now, it was clear, clearly defined, so clearly.

(Pause)

The garden, too, was sharp, lucid, in the rain, in the sun.

(Pause)

My den, too, was sharp, arranged for my purpose … quite satisfactory. *(Pause)*

The house too, was polished, all the banisters were polished, and the stair rods, and the curtain rods.

(Pause)

My desk was polished, and my cabinet.

(Pause)

I was polished. *(Nostalgic)* I could stand on the hill and look through my telescope at the sea. And follow the path of the three-masted schooner, feeling fit, well aware of my sinews, their suppleness, my arms lifted holding the telescope, steady, easily, no trembling, my aim was perfect, I could pour hot water down the spoon-hole, yes, easily, no difficulty, my grasp firm, my command established, my life was accounted for, I was ready for my excursions to the cliff, down the path to the back gate, through the long grass, no need to watch for the nettles, my progress was fluent, after my long struggling against all kinds of usurpers, disreputables, lists, literally lists of people anxious to do me down, and my reputation down, my command was

---

4 **lucid** ['luːsɪd] *(poet)* bright – 8 **banisters** *(Geländer)* – 9 **stair rods** metal sticks used to keep the carpeting on a staircase in place – 11 **cabinet** a piece of furniture with glass doors used for storing small objects of interest – 15 **schooner** ['skuːnə] a fast sailing ship with two or more masts – 15 **sinew** ['sɪnjuː] a strong cord in the body connecting a muscle to a bone – 16 **suppleness** elasticity – 20 **to account for** to give an explanation or a reason for – 22 **fluent** *here:* easy; uninterrupted – 23 **usurper** [juːzɜːpə] a person who seizes power or a position for himself unlawfully or by force – 24 **disreputable** [dɪsˈrepjʊtəbl] person who has a bad character – 25 **to do s.o. down** to destroy s.o.

established, all summer I would breakfast, survey my
landscape, take my telescope, examine the overhanging of
my hedges, pursue the narrow lane past the monastery,
climb the hill, adjust the lens *(he mimes a telescope)*, watch
the progress of the three-masted schooner, my progress was
as sure, as fluent …

(Pause. He drops his arms.)

Yes, yes, you're quite right, it is funny.

(Pause)

Laugh your bloody head off! Go on. Don't mind me. No need
to be polite.

(Pause)

That's right.

(Pause)

You're quite right, it is funny. I'll laugh with you! *(He laughs.)*
Ha-ha-ha! Yes! You're laughing with me, I'm laughing with
you, we're laughing together!

(He laughs and stops.)

(Brightly.) Why did I invite you into this room? That's your
next question, isn't it? Bound to be.

(Pause)

Well, why not, you might say? My oldest acquaintance. My
nearest and dearest. My kith and kin. But surely correspondence would have been as satisfactory … more
satisfactory? We could have exchanged postcards, couldn't
we? What? Views, couldn't we? Of sea and land, city and

---

10 **Laugh your bloody head off!** Laugh yourself silly! – 20 **Bound to be.** Must be, of necessity. – 23 **kith and kin** friends and relatives

village, town and country, autumn and winter … clocktowers … museums … citadels … bridges … rivers …

(Pause)

Seeing you stand, at the back gate, such close proximity, was not at all the same thing.

(Pause)

What are you doing? You're taking off your balaclava … you've decided not to. No, very well then, all things considered, did I then invite you into this room with express intention of asking you to take off your balaclava, in order to determine your resemblance to – some other person? The answer is no, certainly not, I did not, for when I first saw you you wore no balaclava. No headcovering of any kind, in fact. You looked quite different without a head – I mean without a hat – I mean without a headcovering, of any kind. In fact every time I have seen you you have looked quite different to the time before.

(Pause)

Even now you look different. Very different.

(Pause)

Admitted that sometimes I viewed you through dark glasses, yes, and sometimes through light glasses, and on other occasions bare eyed, and on other occasions through the bars of the scullery window, or from the roof, the roof, yes, in driving snow, or from the bottom of the drive in thick fog, or from the roof again in blinding sun, so blinding, so hot, that I had to skip and jump and bounce in order to remain in one

---

4 **proximity** nearness – 10 **with express intention** with the special intention – 25 **drive** a private road to a house – 27 **to skip** to move with quick steps and jumps – 27 **to bounce** to move up and down like a rubber ball

place. Ah, that's good for a guffaw, is it? That's good for a belly laugh? Go on, then. Let it out. Let yourself go, for God's … *(He catches his breath.)* You're crying …

(Pause)

(Moved) You haven't been laughing. You're crying.

(Pause)

You're weeping. You're shaking with grief. For me. I can't believe it. For my plight. I've been wrong.

(Pause)

(Briskly) Come, come, stop it. Be a man. Blow your nose for goodness sake. Pull yourself together.

(He sneezes.) Ah. *(He rises. Sneeze.)* Ah. Fever. Excuse me. *(He blows his nose.)* I've caught a cold. A germ. In my eyes. It was this morning. In my eyes. My eyes.

(Pause. He falls to the floor.)

Not that I had any difficulty in seeing you, no, no, it was not so much my sight, my sight is excellent – in winter I run about with nothing on but a pair of polo shorts – no, it was not so much any deficiency in my sight as the airs between me and my object – don't weep – the change of air, the currents obtaining in the space between me and my object, the shades they make, the shapes they take, the quivering, the eternal quivering – please stop crying – nothing to do with heat-haze. Sometimes, of course, I would take shelter, shelter to compose myself. Yes, I would seek a tree, a cranny

---

1 **guffaw** [gʌˈfɔː] a loud and rude laugh – 2 **belly laugh** a guffaw – 3 **to catch one's breath** to stop breathing for a moment as if surprised or shocked – 7 **grief** deep sorrow – 8 **plight** bad condition or state – 13 **germ** [dʒɜːm] small living thing which causes diseases – 19 **deficiency** [dɪˈfɪʃnsɪ] imperfection – 19 **air** *here (rare)*: gentle wind, a breeze – 21 **current** continuously moving mass of air – 21 **to obtain** *here:* to exist – 22 **to quiver** to tremble – 24 **heat-haze** optical distortion caused by rising hot air – 25 **to compose o.s.** to calm o.s. down – 25 **cranny** a hidden or little-known place

of bushes, erect my canopy and so make shelter. And rest.
(Low murmur) And then I no longer heard the wind or saw
the sun. Nothing entered, nothing left my nook. I lay on my
side in my polo shorts, my fingers lightly in contact with the
blades of grass, the earthflowers, the petals of the earth
flowers flaking, lying on my palm, the underside of all the
great foliage dark, above me, but it is only afterwards I say
the foliage was dark, the petals flaking, then I said nothing, I
remarked nothing, things happened upon me, then in my
times of shelter, the shades, the petals, carried themselves,
carried their bodies upon me, and nothing entered my nook,
nothing left it.

(Pause)

But then, the time came. I saw the wind. I saw the wind,
swirling, and the dust at my back gate, lifting, and the long
grass, scything together … *(Slowly, in horror)* You are
laughing. You're laughing. Your face. Your body.
(Overwhelming nausea and horror) Rocking … gasping …
rocking … shaking … rocking … heaving … rocking … You're
laughing at me! Aaaaahhhh!

(The matchseller rises. Silence)

You look younger. You look extraordinarily … youthful.

(Pause)

You want to examine the garden? It must be very bright, in
the moonlight. *(Becoming weaker)* I would like to join you …
explain … show you … the garden … explain … The plants
… where I run … my track … in training … I was number

---

3 **nook** a sheltered and private place – 5 **petals** [ˈpetlz] the leaf-like (often coloured) divisions of a flower – 6 **to flake** to fall off in little pieces – 7 **foliage** [ˈfəʊlɪdʒ] all the leaves on a tree – 9 **to remark** to say *or:* to notice – 15 **to swirl** to move with twisting turns – 16 **to scythe** [saɪð] to cut with a long, curved knife; here: blades of grass touching one another – 18 **nausea** [ˈnɔːsjə] a feeling of sickness or disgust – 18 **to rock** to move to and fro – 18 **to gasp** to struggle for breath with the mouth open – 19 **to heave** *(of the chest)*: to rise and fall regularly

one sprinter at Howells … when a stripling … no more than a stripling … licked … men twice my strength … when a stripling … like yourself.

(Pause)

(Flatly) The pool must be glistening. In the moonlight. And the lawn. I remember it well. The cliff. The sea. The three-masted schooner.

(Pause)

(With great, final effort– a whisper) Who are you?

FLORA *(off)* Barnabas?

(Pause. She enters.)

Ah, Barnabas. Everything is ready.

(Pause)

I want to show you my garden, your garden. You must see my japonica, my convolvulus … my honeysuckle, my clematis.

(Pause)

The summer is coming. I've put up your canopy for you. You can lunch in the garden, by the pool. I've polished the whole house for you.

(Pause)

Take my hand.

(Pause. The matchseller goes over to her.)

Yes. Oh, wait a moment.

(Pause)

---

2 **stripling** young man – 2 **to lick s.o.** to defeat s.o. – 5 **flatly** in a dull voice – 5 **to glisten** [ˈglɪsn] to shine like something polished

Edward. Here is your tray.

(She crosses to Edward with the tray of matches, and puts it in his hands. Then she and the matchseller start to go out as the curtain falls slowly.)

Biographical Notes

Harold Pinter (1930 – 2008) was born in Hackney, East London, the only son of a Jewish tailor. After attending Hackney Downs Grammar School, Pinter received a grant and began studying at the Royal Academy of Dramatic Art. In 1949, he became a repertory actor; at this time he started writing prose and poetry.

It was not until 1957 that he attempted to write drama: *The Room*, his first play (which is said to have been written in two days), was followed by *The Dumb Waiter* and *The Birthday Party* in the same year. *The Caretaker* (1959) brought him critical acclaim. The 60s and 70s saw Pinter establishing a world-wide reputation through other full-length stage plays, *The Homecoming* (1965), *Old Times* (1971) and *Betrayal* (1978). Later plays include *Family Voices* (1981), *Moonlight* (1993), *Ashes to Ashes* (1996) and *Celebration* (2000).

Pinter also wrote shorter plays (for the stage, radio, and television), the most interesting of which are *A Slight Ache*, *The Lover*, *The Collection*, *Landscape* and *Silence*. His plays are usually divided into three periods "Comedies of menace" (1957 – 1968), "Memory plays" (1968 – 1982) and overtly political plays and sketches (1980 – 2000).

He wrote a large number of screenplay adaptations of other authors' works, among them *The Servant* (1963), The *French Lieutenant's Woman* (1970), *The Trial* (1993) and *Sleuth* (2007).

Harold Pinter received numerous awards and won the Nobel Prize in Literature in 2005.

His plays have often been stamped with the label "Absurd Drama", though Pinter himself would have been the first to object to any attempt to look for a common denominator in his plays.

A Slight Ache was originally conceived as a radio play and broadcast on the BBC Third Programme on 29 July 1959. On 18 January 1961, it was presented at the Arts Theatre, London.

Glossary of Literary Terms

Action: The series of events initiated by the characters in a play. It usually consists of *rising action*, *climax* and *falling action*.
Actor: The person playing a character on stage. His performance is guided by the director and represents an interpretation of the character.
Antagonist: see *Protagonist*.
Character: A person in a play or other literary work.
Climax: Moment at which the action comes to its point of greatest intensity. It marks the turning point of the action.
Dénouement: The resolution of the conflicts in a play.
Dialogue: The conversation between two or more characters.
Director: The person responsible for a performance of a play on stage.
Dramatic irony: The words or actions of a character in a play may carry a meaning unperceived by himself but understood by the audience. The irony lies in the contrast between the meaning intended by the speaker and the added significance seen by others, e.g. when Edward in *A Slight Ache* says about the matchseller, "I should be the same perhaps, in his place", he anticipates the outcome of the play.
Euphemism: The use of an indirect or vague expression for a word which is thought to be offensive or vulgar.
Exposition: That part of the play where background information on the characters and the situation is provided (usually given at the beginning of the play).
Falling action: That part of the play which leads to the resolution of the action. It follows the *climax* and leads to the *dénouement*.
Flat/round character: Flat characters have only one "side". Their behaviour is predictable and they present one single characteristic trait. Round characters are "rounded out",

i.e. they have many "sides" and usually show a certain development in their character.

Irony: A figure of speech where the actual meaning of what is said is hidden behind the obvious statement. It is often used with a humorous or satirical intention.

Metaphor: A figure of speech connecting two different, and basically incompatible, things which have a common ground of comparison, e.g. the quality of continuity and rapid flow in the expression "the river of life".

Monologue: A long speech by one character, heard but not interrupted by the other characters. (Cf. *Soliloquy*).

One-act play: A short play concentrating on a single dramatic situation and aiming at a single dramatic effect. When compared to a full-length play, the structural elements of time, space, character and action appear in a reduced form.

Play within the play: A theatrical performance as part of the play's action, showing the characters of the play as spectators. It is usually employed to confront the audience with their own situation as spectators, e.g. the TV play in James Saunders' *A Slight Accident*.

Plot: The basic structure of the play's action, quite often a causal sequence of events.

Props: Short for "stage properties": articles (e.g. pieces of furniture) used on stage.

Protagonist: The main character of the play; the character around whom the action of the play is centred. His opponent is the antagonist.

Rising action: That part of the play which brings about the complication, i.e. the part in which the opposing forces meet. It follows the *exposition* and leads to the *climax* of the play.

Round character: see *Flat character*.

Scene: Subdivision of a play usually marked by a change of place or the entry or exit of a character. Traditionally: subdivision of an act.

Scenery: The overall picture of the stage comprising *props* and *stage design*.

Setting: The place and time of the action.
Soliloquy: A long speech by one character, which is not meant to be overheard by the other characters and in which he reveals his thoughts to the audience. (Cf. *Monologue*).
Stage design: The decoration of the stage conveying the place, the time and the atmosphere of the play.
Stage direction: That part of the dramatic text which gives information as to how the place and atmosphere of a play are to be imagined or how a speech is to be rendered.
Theatre of the absurd: Dramatic style in which the traditional conceptions of character, plot, time sequence and dialogue are deliberately disregarded. The theatre of the absurd describes human life as purposeless.